CHILDREN'S
ENCYCLOPEDIA
OF NATURAL
DISASTERS

ARCTURUS

Picture Credits:
Every attempt has been made to clear copyright. Should there be any inadvertent omission,
please apply to the publisher for rectification.
Key: b–bottom, t–top, c–center, l–left, r–right

Getty Images: 96–97 JIJI PRESS / Contributor, front cover main, Salvatore Virzi / EyeEm; Shutterstock: Cover insets l–r: structuresxx, Bilanol, aappp, vchal, belish, inside front cover: dani daniar, back cover: Fotos593, inside back cover My Photo Buddy, 1 & 14–15 Fotos593, 4–5 Bilanol, 4t Ali. Fahmi, 4b & 118–119 FotoKina, 5t & 46–47 Christian Roberts–Olsen, 5c David Dreambular, 5b lax15las, 6–7 Thomas Dutour, 6b Everett Collection, 7t, 12–13 & 86–87 Fly_and_Dive, 8–9 & 126 Nido Huebl, 8b BlueRingMedia, 94 Naeblys, 10–11 Olga Danylenko, 11cr & 90br Designua, 11b Ozant, 12c tunasalmon, 12b Tooykrub, 14b, 48c & 110cr VectorMine, 15b Antonio Nardelli, 16–17 Ivan Rivandy, 16c, 90–91, 100bl, 102–103 & 103tr Frans Delian, 18–19 David Pereiras, 18b vchal, 20–21 Tetiana Chernykova, 20tc Cocos.Bounty, 20b gritsalak karalak, 22–23 4.murat, 22b Noska Photo, 24–25 arindambanerjee, 24b Parikh Mahendra N, 25tr thomas koch, 26–27 Olha Tytska, 26b Manoej Paateel, 27t dani daniar, 28–29 F–Focus by Mati Kose, 28b Merkushev Vasiliy, 29c Sally Wallis, 30–31 AJP, 30b pio3, 32–33 sumikophoto, 32b Lucky Team Studio, 34–35 Harry Andresen, 34cr Md. Monzurul Haque, 35br Julia Lopatina, 36–37 Peera_stockfoto, 36bl Thierry Hebbelinck, 38–39 yu_photo, 38b Phoutthavong SOUVANNACHAK, 40–41 MA ANDYANTO, 41b Marcelo F Junior, 42–43 Danita Delimont, 42b Sutipond Somnam, 44–45 Sampajano_Anizza, 45t Juan Enrique del Barrio, 46c Anna LoFi, 47t Logan Bush, 48–49 fotodrobik, 49bl FotograFFF, 50–51 Don Donelson, 50br Haggardous50000, 52–53 & 76bl MNStudio, 53c Konstantin Tronin, 54–55 Serghei Starus, 54b Fabrizio Maffei, 55cr Flash–ka, 56–57 john vlahidis, 56br My Photo Buddy, 57tr Susan Flashman, 58–59 Taras Vyshnya, 58l Steve Desmond, 59cr Stramp, 60–61 Scalia Media, 60c Raland, 61c IM_photo, 62–63 Gabe Shakour, 62bl Benny Marty, 63cr, 64–65 & 65b Ververidis Vasilis, 66–67 fboudrias, 67tr Tomarchio Francesco, 68–69 Morphius Film, 68bl Aleksandar Mijatovic, 69br Phillip Kraskoff, 70–71 Pix_RGB, 70c Belish, 71cr Chrsitian Hartmann, 72–73 Pierre Leclerc, 72bl & 127br Islamic Footage, 72cr Chrispo, 74–75 Dr Morley Read, 74br Anna Klepatckaya, 75br Mati Nitibhon, 76–77 Blanscape, 77cr Josip Pastor, 78–79 LAS Photography, 78b Nature's Charm, 80–81 & 112–113 elRoce, 80bl Edwin Oonk, 80cr Allen.G, 82–83 James Davis Photography, 83cr Roman Sigaev, 84–85 S–F, 85tr MDV Edwards, 88–89 Falcon video, 88cr silviaqs, 92–93 feygraphy, 94–95 Herwin Bahar, 94br Lia Gloss, 96br mTaira, 98–99 Fajrul Islam, 98br & 100–101 fiki j bhayangkara, 102br Youkonton, 104–105 Phubet Juntarungsee, 105 tr The Mariner 4291, 105br PATARA, 106–107 Harvepino, 106cr Syafiq Adnan, 108–109 Camera Kidd, 109br Claudio Caridi, 110–111 VTR2, 111rc John D Sirlin, 112bl El Roce, 113b Captainz, 114–115 & 118br Mia2you, 114cr Yaska, 115t aappp, 116–117 Terry Kelly, 116bl ChameleonsEye, 120–121 ymphotos, 120tr fivepointsix, 121tr IrinaK, 122–123 PradeepGaurs, 122br mehmet ali poyraz, 124–125 Alan LeStourgeon, 124bl Bruce MacQueen, 127t Richard Whitcombe; Wikimedia Commons: 33t Marky7890, 87br Havemeyer Collection,

ARCTURUS

This edition published in 2022 by Arcturus Publishing Limited
26/27 Bickels Yard, 151–153 Bermondsey Street,
London SE1 3HA

Copyright © Arcturus Holdings Limited

Authors: Anne Rooney and Anita Ganeri
Editors: Annabel Savery and Violet Peto
Designer: Lorraine Inglis
Picture research: Lorraine Inglis and Paul Futcher

ISBN: 978-1-3988-2024-1
CH010346NT
Supplier 29, Date 0722, PI 00002385

Printed in China

CHILDREN'S ENCYCLOPEDIA OF NATURAL DISASTERS

CONTENTS

Introduction   4

Chapter 1: Earthquakes   6

What Is an Earthquake?   6
Patchwork of Plates   8
Moving Lands   10
Where Earthquakes Happen   12
How Earthquakes Happen   14
Sea Quakes   16
Watching Out for Quakes   18
On the Ground   20
Human Catastrophe   22
After the Quake   24

Chapter 2: Floods   26

What Is a Flood?   26
Flowing Rivers   28
Flood Patterns   30
Flash Floods   32
Coastal Flooding   34
Flood Damage   36
Human–Made Floods   38
Effects on the Landscape   40
Living with Floods   42
Flood Protection   44

Chapter 3: Forest Fires   46

What Is a Forest Fire?   46
What Is a Fire?   48
How Forest Fires Start   50
Human–Made Forest Fires   52
How Forest Fires Spread   54
Types of Forest Fires   56
Fires and the Landscape   58
Forest Recovery   60
Forest Fires and People   62
Fighting Forest Fires   64

Chapter 4: Volcanoes   66

What Are Volcanoes?   66
How Do Volcanoes Form?   68
Inside a Volcano   70
Shields and Cinders   72
Explosive Volcanoes   74
Mountains and Islands   76
Blown Apart   78
Environmental Effects   80
Mud and Flood   82
Living With Volcanoes   84

Chapter 5: Tsunamis   86

What Is a Tsunami?   86
The Tsunami Zone   88
Earthquakes and Tsunamis   90
Volcanoes and Tsunamis   92
Watery Buildup   94
Minute by Minute   96
Human Catastrophe   98
Sending Help   100
Terrible Aftermath   102
Rebuilding   104

Chapter 6: Hurricanes   106

What Is a Hurricane?   106
Where Hurricanes Happen   108
How Hurricanes Happen   110
Anatomy of a Hurricane   112
Predictable Buildup   114
Wild Winds and Water   116
Riding the Storm   118
People in Danger   120
Helping Out   122
After the Storm   124

GLOSSARY   126

INDEX   128

Introduction

Planet Earth can be wild and unpredictable. The Earth's structure and weather patterns cause dramatic natural events that can be catastrophic for human and animal populations that live in the area. We are going to look at six types of natural disasters, finding out where they happen, why they happen, and how humans are affected by them.

Floods

Water can be dangerous when it arrives in huge quantities. Heavy rainfall, storm surges, and tsunamis can all cause water to flood onto land, damaging or destroying everything in its path.

Earthquakes

During an earthquake, the ground shakes violently and suddenly. In a major earthquake, buildings can be brought down, roads and bridges damaged, and whole towns are affected by the event.

When an earthquake hits, damaged roads and debris make it hard for rescue services to help.

Hurricanes

These tropical storms form over the open ocean. As they sweep inland, their super-strong winds and heavy rainfall can cause extensive damage to cities, towns, and villages. While some can be over in a couple of hours, others can last much longer, and the damage can last a lifetime.

The winds of a hurricane can reach enormous speeds.

Forest Fires

In the hot summer months, many areas of land are at risk of wildfires breaking out. Winds can cause fires to spread dangerously out of control, bringing them within reach of human populations.

When forest fires burn out of control, emergency services may try to limit their spread rather than stop them.

Volcanoes

When hot molten rock is forced to Earth's surface, it can cause a volcanic eruptions, from slow continuous lava flows to enormous explosions that send rock, ash, and smoke high into the air.

Red–hot lava flowing from a volcano cuts a path through anything in its way.

Tsunamis

Tsunamis are giant waves that flow onto and over land. The speed and volume of water can devastate communities in minutes, leading to years of rebuilding and recovery.

The power of a tsunami causes enormous damage to coastal communities.

DID YOU KNOW? Scientists study natural disasters to learn more about how they happen, so that they can help people in the future.

What Is an Earthquake?

During an earthquake, the ground moves or shakes, sometimes very violently. It can bring buildings crashing to the ground and twist or break up roads, train lines, and bridges. For people who experience an earthquake, it can be a terrifying, dangerous event.

Rippling Ground

Shock waves from an earthquake can travel a long way, spreading through the ground just like ripples spread through water. This means that even people who live a long way from where the earthquake happens can be affected. Each year, Earth experiences more than 30,000 earthquakes, although most of these are so small they are completely unnoticed by most people and are detected only by scientists using sensitive measuring instruments.

Earthquakes have happened ever since Earth formed the solid surface that we call the crust. We have historical records of earthquakes throughout human history and geological evidence from earlier times. People long ago did not know what caused earthquakes and often made up legends about them, or they believed their gods were responsible for these terrifying events.

A huge earthquake shook the city of San Francisco in the United States in 1906. It lasted less than a minute but caused enormous damage.

DID YOU KNOW? Shock waves bounce around inside Earth for up to a month after a quake, causing a ringing sound—but you need special equipment to hear it!

Japan is an area often troubled by earthquakes, which can cause tsunamis.

Earthquakes are most dangerous for people when they strike built-up areas. Falling buildings and roads breaking up cause many injuries and deaths.

In 2015, Nepal experienced a violent earthquake, followed by a severe aftershock two weeks later. The epicenter was close to the capital city, Kathmandu.

CASE STUDY: CHILE 1960

In May 1960, an enormous earthquake struck off the coast of southern Chile. It caused tsunamis to travel across the ocean, which resulted in enormous damage and loss of life in Chile and around the Pacific Coast. The earthquake was caused by two of Earth's tectonic plates (see page 8) shifting against each other. The earthquake is the largest recorded in the 20th century.

Patchwork of Plates

If the surface of Earth were a single piece, like the skin of an orange, we wouldn't have any earthquakes. But it is actually many pieces that fit together like a jigsaw puzzle—more like the skin of an orange that has been taken off in pieces and then put back together.

Most tectonic plate boundaries, or faults, are hidden beneath the sea or ground. However, there are some places where fault lines are at the surface.

Earth's Layers

The hard, rocky surface of Earth is called the crust. The crust makes up less than 1% of Earth's thickness. Beneath the crust is a layer of very hot rock called mantle. The mantle can reach temperatures anywhere between 800 °C (1,472 °F) and 3,000 °C (5,432 °F). Beneath the mantle is the outer core, a thick layer of liquid metal. Within the outer core, is the inner core, a ball of metal hotter than the surface of the Sun.

Tectonic Plates

Earth's crust is divided into lots of chunks that fit together to cover the entire Earth's surface. The chunks are called tectonic plates. Tectonic plates meet at fault lines or faults. It is along faults that most earthquakes happen. Most volcanoes are found near the edges of tectonic plates, too.

Beneath Earth's surface is a deep layer of scalding molten rock called mantle.

Six of the large tectonic plates carry land or a mix of land and sea, but much of the Pacific Ocean is on a single, vast plate of its own.

Part of the fault between the North American and Eurasian plates can be seen in Thingvellir National Park in Iceland.

THE ATACAMA TRENCH

Off the west coast of South America is the Atacama (or Peru–Chile) Trench. This is the boundary between the Nazca and South American Plates. Here, the oceanic Nazca plate is forced below the continental South American plate. As the Nazca plate grinds under the plate above, it causes the ground to crack and fold, and this causes earthquakes. The movement of these plates also causes volcanoes.

DID YOU KNOW? At its thickest, Earth's crust is around 60 km (37 mi) deep. The mantle layer is an incredible 2,900 km (1,802 mi) deep!

Moving Lands

Tectonic plates are slowly moving all the time, carried on a layer of thick, gluey, hot rock that gradually creeps around Earth. They move at around 2.5–15 cm (1–6 in) per year, some moving more quickly than others.

Continental Drift

Tectonic plates carry the land that makes up the continents and the sea floor, so as the plates move, the continents gradually shift around the globe. Over many millions of years, the position of landmasses changes. At the moment, the Atlantic Ocean is growing wider, so North America and Europe are moving away from each other.

Three types of faults are created as plates move in different ways. At a convergent (or destructive) fault, tectonic plates push into each other. At a divergent fault, plates move apart over time, and new crust forms between them. At a transform fault, two plates move past each other in opposite directions. However, they cannot slide smoothly, so here pressure builds up. Eventually, the plates slip, and the movement causes an earthquake.

The Himalayas, the tallest mountains in the world, are still being forced up as India moves north at a rate of 5 cm (2 in) per year. The movement of the plates causes many earthquakes.

PANGAEA

Around 250 million years ago, all the landmasses on Earth were grouped together in a single vast continent called Pangaea (meaning "all land"). Although the tectonic plates move very slowly—at about the speed your fingernails grow— their movement is relentless. Over millions of years, they move enough to reshape the continents completely. Before Pangaea, there had been other arrangements of the land. This process has been going on for billions of years.

Mount Everest is the world's highest peak at 8,849 m (29,032 ft) high.

Around 250 million years ago, all the land on Earth was clustered into a single, huge continent named Pangaea.

The movement of the crust is indicated by the red arrows.

Different types of tectonic fault

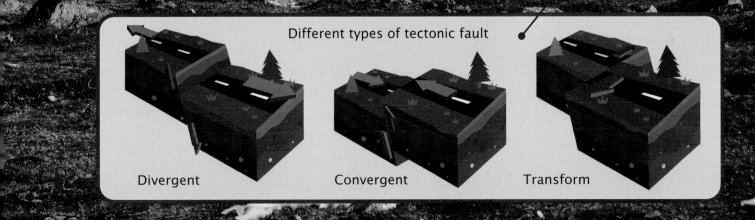

Divergent

Convergent

Transform

DID YOU KNOW? There was once an ocean between India and China. The Tethys Ocean disappeared as Earth's tectonic plates moved.

Where Earthquakes Happen

Almost all earthquakes happen at faults. This means that we can identify earthquake zones: places where earthquakes occur repeatedly and where people can expect them to happen.

On the Edge

The Pacific Ocean is on a large tectonic plate of its own, so there are borders with other plates all the way around the ocean. Most of the boundary of this oceanic plate is vulnerable to earthquakes. There are earthquakes on the west coast of the United States, in parts of western South America, and around Japan, eastern China, and eastern Russia. Some of these areas— Japan, eastern Russia and parts of Central and South America—also have many volcanoes. The rim of the Pacific Plate is called the Ring of Fire because there are so many volcanoes.

Many major cities and communities have been built in areas that are prone to earthquakes. The existence of tectonic plates and fault lines, and their relationship to earthquakes, was not discovered until the 1960s, when many of the areas had already been settled for hundreds of years.

Japan sits on part of the Ring of Fire where two smaller plates are trapped between the Pacific and Eurasian plates.

Ring of Fire

The Ring of Fire is a zone prone to earthquakes and volcanic eruptions that circles the Pacific Ocean.

Today, people design buildings that they hope will withstand earthquakes.

DID YOU KNOW? An enormous 90% of Earth's earthquakes occur around the Pacific Plate, along the Ring of Fire.

In March 2011, an enormous earthquake struck Japan. Some people recorded that the shaking went on for 3 to 5 minutes.

CASE STUDY: KOBE, 1995

Japan is on the junction of multiple tectonic plates and therefore suffers many earthquakes. In January 1995, an earthquake lasting 20 seconds shook the city of Kobe in southern Japan. The ground moved up to 150 cm (59 in) horizontally and 120 cm (47 in) vertically—enough to topple many older buildings and cause serious damage to new ones. More than 6,000 people died, and thousands more were left injured or homeless. After the earthquake, fire raged through the city, stoked by old wooden buildings.

How Earthquakes Happen

Earthquakes happen because pressure builds up where plates are pushing or grinding against each other. The ground does not move smoothly. The plates stick against each other, until finally the plates move and lurch into a new position.

An earthquake can have far-reaching effects as seismic waves spread a long way from the origin of the quake.

Before and After

Foreshocks are tremors (small earthquakes) that happen as the ground begins to shift just before a large earthquake begins. Unfortunately, you cannot tell the difference between a harmless tremor and a foreshock until a main shock follows it.

Aftershocks happen days or even months after a major shock, or main earthquake, as the ground settles into its new position.

Ripple Effect

An earthquake actually happens some way beneath Earth's surface, at a point called the focus. The place on the surface above the focus is called the epicenter. Ripples of energy, called seismic waves, spread out from the focus in all directions, including up and down through the crust.

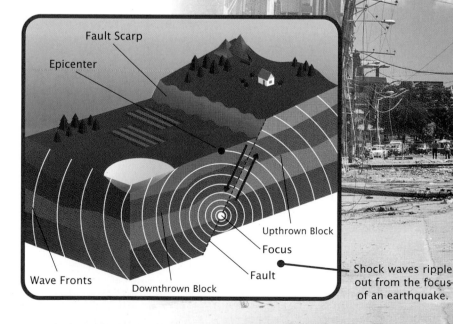

Fault Scarp

Epicenter

Upthrown Block

Focus

Fault

Wave Fronts

Downthrown Block

Shock waves ripple out from the focus of an earthquake.

DID YOU KNOW? The San Andreas Fault on the west coast of the United States is around 1,200 km (800 mi) long and 16 km (10 mi) deep.

The earliest earthquake for which written records remain, destroyed the city of Antioch in Syria (present-day Antakya, Turkey) in May 526 CE. The quake struck when the city was full of crowds that had come to celebrate a religious festival. The quake caused oil lamps to fall, sparking a fire that raged through the ruins, killing many people who had survived the quake itself. Records suggest 250,000 people may have died in the city and surrounding area.

In April 2016, an earthquake struck off the coast of Ecuador. The earthquake was caused by the movement of the Nazca plate sliding under the South American plate.

The threat of aftershocks makes rescue work dangerous.

Sea Quakes

Many earthquakes happen under the sea. Fault lines run all around the Pacific Ocean, along the middle of the Atlantic Ocean, and through the Indian Ocean and Mediterranean Sea.

Reaching Land

Even if the epicenter of an earthquake is out at sea, the seismic waves can travel far inland. The shock waves from a very large earthquake can go all around the world, though they get weaker as they get farther from the focus of the earthquake. The shock waves may still be strong enough when they reach land to topple buildings. In Europe, a fault runs through the Mediterranean Sea and comes close to southern Italy. Earthquakes near Italy are often felt on the land. In 1908, around 120,000 people were killed by an earthquake in the sea between Italy and Sicily.

Tsunamis

Earthquakes under the sea often cause tsunamis, massive waves that flood huge areas of land. Tsunamis are frequently responsible for more deaths than falling buildings when an earthquake happens beneath or near the sea. A tsunami can even start on a large lake or river. As the ground beneath the sea moves, a vast body of water drops down or is forced up or sideways, creating gigantic waves that travel in all directions. When the waves approach shallow water, they grow very tall—up to 30 m (100 ft)—and then they rush inland as a terrible flood, destroying everything. As the wave retreats again, it drags people and wreckage out to sea.

The Indian Ocean tsunami waves were just 1 m (3 ft) high when in the open ocean. When they reached the shore, some had built to 15 m (49 ft) high.

DID YOU KNOW? Before a tsunami, the sea can draw far out, revealing the ocean floor.

In 2018, a tsunami swept into the Indonesian city of Palu triggered by an underwater earthquake. Many were killed and buildings and homes destroyed.

Two mosques survived the disaster in Palu that destroyed many other buildings.

CASE STUDY:
INDIAN OCEAN, 2004

In December 2004, a massive earthquake under the Indian Ocean caused a tsunami that flooded lands all around the ocean. Its worst effects were in Indonesia, Thailand, India, and Sri Lanka. As part of the seabed near Sumatra was thrust upward, vast amounts of seawater were displaced, rushing outward in waves that spread over 4,500 km (2,796 mi) during a period of seven hours. At intervals of 5 and 40 minutes, waves swept inland, destroying towns, businesses, and communities.

Watching Out for Quakes

In the past, foreshocks were the only warning people had that an earthquake might be about to happen. Nowadays, scientists have many ways of watching for possible earthquakes—but we can still be surprised by a quake that gives no warning.

Watching Waves

A seismograph is an instrument that picks up movement of the ground, including shifts too slight for us to feel. In a simple seismograph, a suspended pen draws a line on a piece of paper. As the ground moves, the shaking makes the line wobble—large spikes in the line show significant tremors. Modern seismographs use computers that immediately perform calculations from the recordings.

A single seismograph can only show the distance between the seismograph machine and the epicenter of a quake—it cannot say exactly where the epicenter is. The epicenter could be anywhere within the distance recorded by the seismograph. However, when information from three seismographs in different places is shared, it is possible to pinpoint the epicenter of a quake.

In countries that experience earthquakes frequently, everyone learns important earthquake safety drills.

A mechanical seismograph is used to monitor ground movement.

DID YOU KNOW? By learning emergency drills, we can make our actions faster if an emergency does happen.

ANIMALS AND EARTHQUAKES

There are many tales of animals reacting to an earthquake long before people can feel any tremors. In China and Japan, there are stories of snakes coming out of the ground, of dogs howling, roosters crowing, and even pandas holding their heads in their paws. Before the tsunami that struck Thailand in 2004, elephants headed inland to the forest before the tsunami was visible. Animals appear to be more sensitive to ground movement than people. Sometimes watching animals can save human lives. In 1975, the Chinese city of Haicheng was evacuated because its animals were behaving strangely. Several hours later, a massive earthquake struck the city.

A mother explains to her children how to protect themselves in an earthquake by getting under the table. They also have emergency supplies ready in bags.

On the Ground

An earthquake is a terrifying experience for anyone who is caught up in it. The shaking itself lasts only a few seconds, but the damage can be catastrophic.

During an Earthquake

The first warning of an earthquake for most people is the foreshocks, which cause windows to rattle and small objects to move around. Sometimes, though, there is no warning, and the ground suddenly lurches dramatically. Buildings crack and may fall down, and roads, bridges, and train lines twist and break apart. Damaged structures continue to fall after the shaking stops. Where there are no buildings to fall, the quake is not usually as dangerous for people.

Measuring Earthquakes

In order to study and compare earthquakes, seismologists have developed ways of measuring them. There are two methods of measuring the intensity or severity of an earthquake.

The Richter scale registers the amount of ground movement an earthquake causes. Quakes that register below 3 cannot be felt by people. A severe earthquake measures between 7 and 7.9, and a very severe earthquake measures over 8. Although earthquakes over 10 could occur, none above 9.5 has ever been recorded.

The Modified Mercalli Intensity scale records levels of damage as a way of comparing earthquakes. The scale goes from I, Instrumental (detected only by scientific instruments), to X, Extreme (with the ground moving in waves, and all structures destroyed).

Earthquakes can cause floods and landslides that damage roads and other infrastructure.

Modified Mercalli Scale

I II III IV V VI VII VIII IX X

In July 1976, an earthquake measuring 7.5 on the Richter scale shook the Chinese city of Tangshan. It destroyed 85% of the buildings, and at least 242,000 people were killed. In addition to this, 700,000 people are thought to have been injured. On the Mercalli scale, the earthquake is thought to have reached X (extreme) in the city of Tangshan and VIII (severe) in the surrounding area. The city had not been built to withstand earthquakes, because the fault that caused the quake was unknown at the time.

As soon as an earthquake hits, the emergency services start to calculate where the epicenter is.

It's not only transportation systems that can be damaged, but communication, water, and energy services too.

DID YOU KNOW? A huge 7.1 magnitude aftershock hit China just hours after the main Tangshan earthquake!

Human Catastrophe

The dangers to people of being caught in an earthquake last much longer than the few seconds during that the ground shakes. More tremors often follow the main earthquake, and quakes often cause fires or floods.

Dangerous Cities

When an earthquake strikes a built-up area, people may be hit by falling debris, caught in collapsing buildings, or trapped under rubble. In a modern city, falling glass and masonry from high-rise buildings pose a threat to people, and collapsing ground can crush underground train networks and bring down road and rail bridges. Poorly built buildings and overpopulated cities can lead to a high death toll. This is a particular danger in South America, the Middle East, and the Indian subcontinent.

As the ground settles, aftershocks can topple buildings and other structures made unsafe by the main quake. Aftershocks may happen within hours or days, but can occur up to several months after the earthquake.

Often, an earthquake triggers further disasters. In towns and cities, damage to gas and electricity supplies can lead to fires. Landslides, avalanches, mudslides, and rockfalls are common where there is unstable ground, deep snow, or wet land.

Trained search and rescue dogs help emergency teams to find people trapped in debris.

22

The city of San Francisco in California, USA, lies on the San Andreas fault, a boundary between tectonic plates that runs up the western coast of the United States. In April 1906, 477 km (296 mi) of the fault ruptured in a huge earthquake that rocked the city for between 40 and 60 seconds. After the devastation of the quake, the city was engulfed in an unstoppable fire that razed it to the ground. Historians now believe that more than 3,000 people died in the quake and the fire.

Aftershocks are a serious danger for rescue workers and for people who are trapped or injured and awaiting help.

DID YOU KNOW? An earthquake close to the present–day city of Izmir, Turkey, in 1688, shook the ground so much that the surface dropped by 30 cm (1 ft)!

After the Quake

The aftermath of an earthquake can last for decades, especially for those who lose family members, their home, or livelihood.

Immediate Aftermath

Right after a major earthquake, the affected area is in chaos. There are often no communication networks because telephone links and electricity supplies have been lost. There may be no hospitals, no emergency services, and no way of getting even basic medical supplies, food, and water to survivors. People who have survived the devastation of the quake may be left injured, without food or shelter, or in danger from heat or exposure because they have no protection from the weather and no appropriate clothing.

When an earthquake struck Port-au-Prince, Haiti, in 2010, nearly 300,000 homes were damaged or destroyed, and 1.5 million people were made homeless.

Wrecked Communities

After a major earthquake, many people are bereaved or left homeless, and even more have their way of life destroyed. The local community is robbed of schools, hospitals, workplaces, and all the infrastructure of normal life. Individuals may be suffering from injuries sustained in the quake or traumatized by loss, and face a life of struggling to cope with what has happened.

When an earthquake strikes, people can lose everything: family, homes, and possessions.

DID YOU KNOW? Following the earthquake in Haiti in 2010, 35,000 people were still living in camps in 2020, ten years later.

People living in emergency camps often have to rely on other people for food.

Following Haiti's 2010 earthquake, temporary shelters were constructed for the huge amounts of people made homeless by the disaster.

CASE STUDY: SPITAK, ARMENIA, 1988

In December 1988, an earthquake registering 6.8 on the Richter scale destroyed the Armenian city of Spitak and damaged surrounding cities and villages. Because of the building methods used, schools and hospitals were among the worst hit, and many children died. International aid workers and advisors helped in the rescue and rebuilding work, but the Armenians could not afford to make some of the changes recommended. The city has been rebuilt, but it could still suffer severe damage in another earthquake.

What Is a Flood?

A flood happens when water from a river or the sea covers dry land. Heavy rains can turn gently flowing rivers into terrifying torrents that sweep across the landscape, submerging land under deep, muddy water. Powerful storms and giant waves can send seawater cascading over low-lying coasts.

Floods alter the landscape by eroding soil, carrying it away, and dumping it elsewhere.

Killer Floods

Over the centuries, millions of people have died in floods. A single, huge flood can bring catastrophe, killing millions of people. Floods are more frequent than other natural disasters, and they cause as much damage to property as all other natural disasters put together.

There are three main types of floods: river floods, flash floods, and coastal floods. Most floods happen on rivers, when excess water overflows from a river onto flat land called the floodplain. The most devastating floods happen along the world's great rivers. Flash floods happen suddenly when intense rain falls over a small area. Coastal floods happen when storms and tsunamis raise the sea level above the level of the coast.

Floodwater damages buildings, electricity cables, and other infrastructure.

DID YOU KNOW? Floods can happen in the desert!

Fast-flowing floodwater can wash away buildings, cars, trees, and roads.

The soil on river floodplains is extremely fertile, making them good places to grow crops.

CASE STUDY: THE BIBLICAL FLOOD

In the Bible, God sends a great flood that covers the whole Earth. Only a man named Noah and his family survive. There are many other similar stories of great floods. They may be based on a flood that happened about 5,000 years ago in modern-day Iraq, where archaeologists have found a thick layer of sediment deposited by massive flooding.

Flowing Rivers

Before looking at why floods happen on rivers, it is useful to understand how rivers flow. The water on Earth is constantly circulating between the oceans, the atmosphere, and the land. This circulation of water is called the water cycle.

Water Cycle

Water evaporates (changes to a gas) from the oceans and land and rises up into the atmosphere. As the gas rises and cools, it forms water droplets that fall as rain and other precipitation. The drops run off the land, forming streams and rivers that flow back to the sea.

Water on Land

Rain either soaks into the ground or flows across the ground, when it is called runoff. The amount of water that soaks in or runs off depends on the type of ground, how wet the ground is, and how heavy the rain is. Water soaks into some soils faster than others. For example, it soaks quickly into sandy soil but very slowly into clay. If rain falls so heavily that not all of it can soak in, the surplus rain sits on top of the soil or runs off it, downhill. When the ground becomes saturated (soaked with water), all the rain runs off.

When the river reaches lowland areas, the river naturally meanders (bends) from side to side. Over time, the meandering river slowly cuts a wide valley.

The water cycle is constant: rain falls, rivers flow, and oceans evaporate.

DID YOU KNOW? Heavy floodwater in Texas, USA, in 2002, carved a 2.2 km (1.4 mi) long, more than 7 m (23 ft) deep canyon in the earth in just three days!

In July 2021, heavy rains fell across areas of western Europe. In areas with the highest rainfall, two months of rain fell in just 24 hours. People in Germany, Belgium, and the Netherlands awoke to flash floods, and many were evacuated. Because the rains fell overnight, many were unprepared: Around 200 people were killed and thousands more were injured. The floodwater surged along the Meuse and Roer rivers, and a dam on the Rur River was breached. When the floodwaters receded, towns were damaged and covered with thick river mud and silt.

As rain runs off fields and it takes soil particles with it, this makes muddy floods on roads.

Some of the soil and rock transported by the river is deposited. The flat area around the river is called the floodplain.

Flood Patterns

Rivers often flood at the same time each year. These seasonal floods are caused by high rainfall or by melting snow in major mountain ranges. Rains fall at different times of the year in different climates. In South Asia, floods are caused by heavy summer rains called monsoons. The amount of water flowing down rivers can increase by about twenty times during this wet season.

Chances of Flooding

The severity of a flood is measured by how often such a flood happens. A ten-year flood happens, on average, once every ten years. A hundred-year flood on the same river, which would happen on average every 100 years, would be far more serious. A person living alongside this river would probably only experience such a serious flood once in their lifetime.

A flood does not happen as soon as it starts to rain. It takes time for the water to find its way into rivers and to build up. Then a surge of floodwater moves down the river. At a particular point on a river, the water level gradually rises, peaks, and subsides again. It may take many hours or even days before the river floods farther downstream, and there can be floods far from where the rain that caused the flood actually fell.

Tropical cyclones create one–off floods because they drop huge amounts of rain in a short time.

The monsoon season lasts from June to September. These heavy rains can have devastating effects, causing thousands of deaths and making millions of people homeless.

These floods in the Indian town of Alleppey were caused by the monsoon rains of 2018. That year's monsoon was responsible for the worst floods in the region of Kerala, India in nearly a century.

CASE STUDY: FLOODING IN CHINA

Southern China has a summer monsoon, when a large volume of rain falls in a few months. The area is drained by two enormous rivers, the Huang Ho (Yellow River) and the Chiang Jang (Yangtze). Monsoon floods happen regularly along these rivers. When the rains are heavier than normal, the flooding can be catastrophic. In 1931, weather events caused water levels to rise up to 16 m (53 ft) above normal. It is thought that these floods caused as many as 4 million deaths.

DID YOU KNOW? The rugged terrain of the Pacific Northwest of the USA was carved by mega floods in the last ice age, 13,000 to 18,000 years ago.

Flash Floods

A flash flood is a sudden, short flood. Most flash floods are caused by extremely heavy rainfall from slow-moving storm clouds. This causes a huge volume of water to land in one place in a short space of time. The water takes the quickest route downhill, which may be along a narrow valley or through a town or city.

In deserts, as in towns, the ground can be hard, and water cannot be absorbed into it. Sudden heavy rainfall can cause dangerous flash flooding.

Storm Clouds

The intense rain that causes flash floods comes from storm clouds that can be more than 8 km (5 mi) tall. The clouds grow when warm, humid air rises. Inside the clouds, air swirls up and down, carrying water droplets with it. The droplets grow larger until they fall from the base of the cloud. Sometimes the whole cloud collapses, releasing hundreds of thousands of tons of water in a few minutes. This is known as a cloudburst.

Where Flash Floods Happen

Flash floods often happen on rivers that are too small to cope with the sudden flow of large volumes of water. Flash floods also occur when intense rain falls onto waterlogged ground, but they can also happen on dry ground if the rain is heavy enough. This is how they happen in deserts. Flash floods can happen in towns and cities when the rain is so heavy that drains cannot carry it away fast enough. Flash floods are usually localized: They affect just a single stream or street.

Highly populated places are at risk of severe damage by flash floods.

In August 2004, the English seaside village of Boscastle was devastated by a flash flood. In the afternoon of a very warm day, a series of giant thunderstorms formed in the area. The storms dropped 75 mm (3 in) of rain in just two hours. Two rivers carried the water into the village, forming a roaring torrent up to 3 m (10 ft) deep in the streets. Houses were destroyed and cars swept out to sea, but luckily nobody was killed.

In southern Utah, USA, the ground is hard and water runs quickly off, forming flash floods. A storm can be a long distance away from where the flash flooding occurs.

DID YOU KNOW? Water doesn't have to be deep to be dangerous—you could be knocked down in 15 cm (6 in) of fast-moving floodwater.

Coastal Flooding

The land along many coasts is only a little way above sea level. In some places, it is actually below sea level, and the sea is held back by natural banks or artificial barriers. In these areas, a rise in sea level can cause water to pour inland, causing severe flooding.

A rise in sea levels may be caused by storms and high winds combined with high tides, and also by tsunamis. Seawater can also flow up estuaries, causing flooding far inland.

Storm Surges

Most coastal flooding is caused by storm systems such as tropical cyclones. These cause a rise in water levels called a storm surge. In a storm system, the air pressure is lower than normal. In other words, the pressure of the air pushing down on that part of Earth's surface is less than average. The lower air pressure allows the water underneath to bulge upward slightly to form a storm surge. The highest storm surges are caused by tropical cyclones. They can be 5 m (16 ft) high, or more.

Embankments are built up at times when the water level is high.

CASE STUDY: NEW ORLEANS, 2005

In August 2005, the city of New Orleans on the southeast coast of the United States was badly flooded by the storm surge from Hurricane Katrina. The surge pushed seawater into a lake next to the city, raising its level 2 m (6 ft) above normal. Levees (flood barriers) collapsed, and the water flowed into the city, much of which is below sea level.

DID YOU KNOW? When Hurricane Katrina hit the US coast in 2005, around 80% of New Orleans was flooded.

Low-lying coastal areas are often highly populated. Millions of people live in cities that could be affected by coastal flooding.

The streets of Venice are regularly underwater at high tide leading up to winter, and during storms. Over recent years, floods have been getting worse.

Areas at Risk

Parts of some major cities, such as London, are only a little way above sea level. Low-lying islands can be completely submerged in a coastal flood. The Italian city of Venice is built on 118 small islands, and the city regularly floods during storms. More than half of the Netherlands is below or at sea level. The country has introduced many flood management schemes to keep its citizens safe.

Flood Damage

Floodwater can cause a huge amount of damage. Fast-flowing water picks up and carries along anything in its path: cars, boats, branches, litter, mud. The power of a tsunami or storm surge can damage housing and devastate communities.

The Power of Water

Floodwaters can move extremely quickly: Tsunamis rush across the ocean at around 800 kph (500 mph). Flash floods, storm surges, and a river bursting its banks can all cause fast-flowing water to burst into communities. The force of the torrent can be enough to smash buildings apart, ripping off doors and breaking windows, lifting cars, sweeping along benches, pulling up trees and snapping branches. All the broken material is gathered and swept along by the rushing water, making it even more dangerous and destructive.

In southern Laos, tropical storms can bring torrential rains, which cause rivers to burst their banks.

What's Left?

After a flood, the community is left with broken buildings, roads, bridges and cars, and damaged power and communication lines. Chemical containers and sewers can be damaged, leaking harmful substances into the water. When the floodwaters flow away, silt and sand carried along by the river settles on everything, and huge amounts of debris are left behind. Disease spreads through unclean water, and newly-homeless communities can be further affected by outbreaks of illnesses, such as typhoid and malaria.

Serious damage can be seen in Belgium weeks after heavy flooding in 2021.

In 2000, Mozambique experienced three weeks of heavy rain followed by a tropical cyclone that swept inland across the north of the country. The floodwaters destroyed water pumping facilities, leaving cities without access to clean water. Thousands of people were left homeless and diseases such as cholera and dysentery spread through temporary camps. Schools and hospitals were destroyed, livestock and crops were lost, along with fishing boats and equipment. In a country that was already poor, damage to housing, crops and farmland, and coastal businesses was devastating.

Fast-flowing river water can rush across the land, washing mud and debris into towns and communities.

DID YOU KNOW? Around the world, floods cause $40 billion worth of damage each year.

Human-Made Floods

The vast majority of floods happen naturally, but sometimes people cause floods. Most are accidental. They happen when stored water escapes from behind dams or embankments. In the future, climate change will also lead to more floods on rivers and coasts. Human beings will be responsible for these floods because it is our use of fossil fuels that is the main cause of global warming.

We build dams on rivers to store water for water supplies and irrigation, to produce hydroelectricity, and also to prevent flooding.

Dam Bursts

In a few rare cases, dams have collapsed, causing deadly floods in the valleys below. Dams can collapse because they are poorly designed, because they are damaged by powerful earthquakes, or because floodwater flows over the top of the dam, eroding the foundations at the base. Some experts believe that giant flood-control dams are disasters waiting to happen.

Sometimes we flood land deliberately. For example, the land behind a dam is flooded permanently by a reservoir. Building dams stops the natural flow of water down a river, which can damage wildlife habitats along the river bank.

In 2018, a new dam being built in Laos collapsed, flooding local villages.

The Kurobe Dam is the highest in Japan at 186 m (610 ft). It was built in 1963 and supports a hydropower plant.

CASE STUDY: ST. FRANCIS DAM FAILURE, 1928

The St. Francis Dam in California, USA, was completed in 1926. It was built to supply water to the city of Los Angeles. The reservoir was filled in 1928. Cracks soon appeared in the concrete, but engineers were not concerned because they thought that the dam was still structurally sound. A few days later, the dam collapsed. A wall of water 37 m (124 ft) high crashed down the valley and through several towns. More than 400 people died. Last minute design changes, unstable rock, and poorly mixed concrete all contributed to the disaster.

DID YOU KNOW? Today, there are so many dams that only around 20% of the world's rivers flow uninterrupted to the ocean.

Effects on the Landscape

Floods change the shape of the landscape along rivers and coasts. During a flood, erosion increases and rivers carry and deposit more sediment. Erosion cuts into the riverbed and banks, and sediment is dropped on the floodplain. Floods can even cause a river to change course completely by cutting a new channel.

Erosion

Fast-flowing floodwater has incredible power. It picks up rocks and pushes them along. The rocks crash into the riverbed and banks, eroding them even more. In flash floods, huge boulders can be washed downstream. In steep valleys, the erosion weakens the valley sides, causing landslides and mudslides. In very dry areas, where the soil is loose, torrential summer rain cuts deep gullies into the landscape.

Deposition

During a flood, river water turns brown because of the huge amount of sediment it is carrying. Some of this sediment settles on the riverbed, making the river more shallow. When river water flows over a floodplain, it drops sediment, covering the plain in silt or mud. Deposited sediment can also build up natural embankments on the riverside. When the river reaches the sea, sediment is deposited, forming a delta.

As riverbanks are eroded by fast flood waters, anything built near the river may become unstable. If floods are expected, people can be evacuated to safe areas.

At the delta of the Parnaiba River, Brazil, sand is washed down the river and deposited at the river's mouth.

VEGETATION STOPS EROSION

Plants help to reduce the amount of run-off from the land. Their roots allow water to soak into the soil. Roots also take up some of the water, helping to dry out the soil. Some water that lands on plants evaporates back into the air. Where vegetation is cleared, heavy rain runs off the land as soon as it falls, causing flash floods that strip away the loose soil.

As floodwaters rush past eroding the riverbed, they make the land above more unstable. This land can then slip and fall, causing a landslide.

DID YOU KNOW? In 1999, heavy rains in Venezuela caused floods and mudslides that buried whole towns under tons of mud.

Living with Floods

Hundreds of millions of people live on floodplains and in coastal areas that are at risk from flooding. Why do people live in flood-risk areas, and how do floods affect their lives?

Good for Growing

The main advantage of living on floodplains is that they are good places for growing crops. The sediment deposited on floodplains during floods is rich in the minerals that plants need. The river is also convenient for irrigating the crops. However, when floods come at an unseasonal time or are higher than usual, they can destroy a whole year's crop.

For centuries, rice farmers in Asia have relied on floods along huge rivers such as the Ganges and Mekong. The fields, called paddies, have earth banks around them. During monsoon floods, the floodwater fills the paddies. The earth banks ensure that the floodwater remains there.

Farmers plant rice in paddies. This method of farming would not be possible without regular floods.

DID YOU KNOW? Farmers in Egypt farmed the rich Nile floodplain for thousands of years. It flooded every year in August.

In some countries, people have no choice but to live with the threat of floods, because the only land available to them is on a floodplain.

When floods come, these houses in Bangladesh stay above the floodwater because they are built on tall stilts.

CASE STUDY: FLOODING IN BANGLADESH

Bangladesh lies in an area of the world hit by regular river flooding and tropical cyclones. Most of the country is made up of the floodplains and deltas of three huge rivers: the Ganges, the Brahmaputra, and the Meghna. Millions of farmers live in these flood-prone areas. In 1991, a cyclone with a 6 m (20 ft) storm surge hit Bangladesh, causing severe flooding and high winds. About 140,000 people died, more than 1 million homes were lost, and millions of tons of crops were ruined.

43

Flood Protection

For thousands of years, people have been trying to protect their homes and crops from floods. Today, there are two main methods of flood protection. We can build structures that keep water from escaping from rivers or spreading inland from the coast. We can also reduce the amount of water flowing down a river, so that the water is less likely to overflow.

Building Flood Barriers

The simplest form of river flood protection is an embankment or wall on each bank of the river. This stops floodwater from overflowing onto the floodplain.

Water that would cause floods farther downstream can also be diverted along channels into other rivers or into hollows to form temporary lakes. Water can also be allowed to spread onto parts of the floodplain to keep it from overflowing in other places.

Dams are sometimes built to prevent rivers from flooding. The reservoir stores the rush of floodwater from upstream and releases it slowly, preventing a surge downstream. The reservoir must be carefully managed, so that floodwater does not make it overflow.

The Thames Flood Barrier in east London closes its gates to prevent storm surges from flowing up the Thames to low-lying areas of the city.

CASE STUDY: NORTH SEA, 1953

In January 1953, high winds in the North Sea caused an enormous storm surge. It flooded a huge area of the Netherlands, causing 1,800 deaths and much damage. It also flooded parts of eastern England, where 300 lives were lost and 24,000 homes damaged. Both countries took steps to protect themselves from future surges. The Oosterscheldekering is a vast barrier that protects part of The Netherlands from storm surges. It is part of a bigger project called the Delta Works. The Thames Barrier in London, UK, is part of the United Kingdom's flood protection.

A dam forms part of the Eresma River in Spain.

Protect or Not?

Some flood experts argue that flood protection is a bad idea. Keeping a river from overflowing onto its floodplain simply pushes more water downstream, making flooding more likely there. Flood protection also encourages people to build houses on floodplains, which could be dangerous if a really large flood comes along. These experts say we should work with nature rather than against it.

The barrier closes when dangerously high tides are forecast. It stretches 520 m (1,700 ft) across the river and is made of ten metal gates.

DID YOU KNOW? The Oosterscheldekering is 9 km (5.5 mi) long and made from 65 huge concrete pillars!

What Is a Forest Fire?

The sight of a fire sweeping furiously through a forest is both frightening and spectacular. Forest fires (also called wildfires) are devastating events. Their intense heat burns leaves and branches to a crisp before making them explode, roaring, and crackling, into flames.

Giant flames leap high into the air, along with columns of thick, black smoke.

A Fiery Path

Even the biggest wildfire starts as a tiny spark. If the vegetation is dry enough, the spark quickly grows into an inferno. Flames spread in all directions, burning everything in their path. They damage and kill trees, incinerate plants on the forest floor, and even kill roots under the ground. Buildings in the way are also burned. Any unfortunate people or animals who become trapped between the fast-moving flames may be killed. When the flames are gone, a charred, smoking wasteland is left behind.

Animals living in fire-prone forests can sometimes outrun the flames, but may be harmed by smoke.

A NATURAL CYCLE

Lightning has been starting wildfires throughout history. Layers of charcoal in rocks tell us that there were devastating fires millions of years ago. Blackened tree rings in very old trees show that natural forest fires are regular events in some places. Although fires can be damaging, they are not always bad news. Fire clears out old trees and allows new ones to grow. There is a natural cycle of fire and regrowth. In fact, some species of tree could not survive without regular fires.

DID YOU KNOW? In 2019, there were around over 80,000 forest fires in Brazil.

Firefighters tackle fires from the ground and from the air.

Where and Why?

Wildfires happen in places where hot summer weather dries out dense vegetation. They happen more often during droughts. The dry vegetation catches fire easily and allows the fire to spread rapidly. Fire affects both coniferous and deciduous forests. It can also burn across grasslands, scrub, and heather moorlands. Most wildfires are started accidentally by people, but some are started naturally by lightning.

In the biggest fires, whirling tornadoes are created by the rapidly rising heat.

What Is a Fire?

Before we can investigate how forest fires burn and how firefighters combat them, we need to understand what exactly fire is. A fire is made up of glowing, red-hot material and often flames. These give off heat and normally produce smoke.

The Fire Triangle

A fire must have three things to keep burning: fuel, heat, and oxygen. These three things make up the "fire triangle." A fuel is any material that burns—not just the fuels we use for heating, in cars, and so on. Fuel must be heated before it will burn, and this heat must be provided for a fire to start. Once a fire is burning, however, it produces its own heat, and so it can keep on burning. Oxygen comes from the air, so a fire needs a supply of air.

O_2 OXYGEN

HEAT

FUEL

The triangle shows that the elements on all three sides must be there for the fire to continue burning.

Flames and Smoke

Plant matter, such as wood and leaves, is made up of several substances, including cellulose and lignin. When plant matter is heated, these substances begin to break up. Chemical reactions between parts of the plant matter and the air release energy as heat and light, which we see as flames. The material that remains is mostly carbon. Some tiny bits of unburned carbon are carried into the air. These mix with the air to form smoke. Water from the plant material boils in the heat, making steam that rises with the smoke.

STOPPING FIRE

If you remove one of the three sides of the fire triangle (fuel, heat, or oxygen), the fire cannot keep burning. So if the fuel runs out, the heat is taken away; or if the oxygen supply is cut off the fire goes out. These are the basic ways of fighting fire. Firefighters can stop a fire by taking away fuel, cooling it with water, or smothering it with foam.

48

Fire happens when a material burns. Burning is also called combustion.

The tree bark is glowing as the carbon in it burns.

Firefighters try to keep the fire from spreading by beating down the edges and preventing it from reaching new fuel materials.

DID YOU KNOW? Nearly 85% of the wildfires in the United States are caused by human actions.

How Forest Fires Start

Two conditions are needed for a forest fire to start. First, the forest fuel (the trees, other plants, and dead matter on the ground) must be dry. Second, there must a source of heat to ignite the fuel and start the fire.

Where Fires Happen

Forest fires happen most regularly in parts of the world where winters are cool and wet and summers are hot and dry. This type of climate provides good growing conditions for trees and other plants, so there is plenty of vegetation around. But in the summer, the vegetation can dry out. Two of the world's wildfire hotspots are the west of North America and southeast Australia, where there are thousands of fires every year. However, in severe droughts, fires can even rage in tropical rain forests, where conditions are normally too wet for fires to start.

What Ignites Fires?

Fires are either started by natural events or by people, either accidentally or deliberately. By far the most common natural fire starter is lightning. It is the major cause of fire in remote areas. Fires are occasionally started by volcanic eruptions. Another cause is the buildup of heat from rotting vegetation on the forest floor, known as spontaneous combustion.

Drought makes fires far more likely. With less rainfall, the vegetation becomes dry and will burn easily.

When lightning strikes a tree, a huge electric current flows through the tree. This heats the tree very quickly, which can make it ignite.

Fires are essential to the ecosystems in the Everglades National Park, Florida, USA. They are usually started by lightning.

CASE STUDY:
FIRE IN FRANCE

Summers in the south of France are very hot and very dry. These conditions dry out the forests. Hundreds of fires start every year, and major fires burn every six years or so. The fires are made worse by the mistral: a strong northwesterly wind that often blows through the valleys during the summer. This fans the flames, allowing the fires to spread dangerously fast.

DID YOU KNOW? There are around 3 million flashes of lightning every day around the world!

Human-Made Forest Fires

Most wildfires are caused accidentally, but some are started deliberately, either for land management or to reduce fire risk. In Australia, the majority of forest fires are started by people.

Accidental Fires

Forest fires are started accidentally in many ways. A common cause is campfires that get out of control or that are not put out properly. Discarded matches and cigarettes, and domestic waste fires also start fires. Sparks from trains and logging machines can ignite fires if they fall into dry leaves and other plant matter on the forest floor.

A surprising number of forest fires are started deliberately. Some are lit for revenge, perhaps to try and burn down property close to the forest. People also light them simply for the thrill of seeing a fire.

Fire for Land Management

One of the major causes of forest fires today is slash-and-burn land clearance (also called shift cultivation). This is undertaken in rain forests, such as the Amazon rain forest, to clear land for crops and cattle. During a drought, these fires can easily get out of control, causing major damage.

CASE STUDY: INDONESIAN FIRES, 1997

In 1997, the tropical forests of Indonesia were being cleared by farmers and companies who wanted more land to grow palm oil and trees for papermaking. That year, the forests were dry because the seasonal rains had failed to arrive. Many of the fires used to clear the land got out of control. Some burned for months before being extinguished by the rain. Smoke from the fires affected many cities in Malaysia, Indonesia, and Singapore, and millions of people were treated for breathing problems.

Campfires are a major cause of forest fires. They must be carefully controlled to keep fire from spreading to nearby vegetation.

Drones can help firefighters monitor fires from the air.

In the USA, wildfire season lasts from June to September. In 2015, 40,000 km² (15,500 mi²) burned during the wildfire season.

DID YOU KNOW? Burning small sections of land is an ancient practice that clears dry fuel materials, preventing bigger wildfires from spreading.

How Forest Fires Spread

Heat produced by a fire moves by convection (hot air currents) and radiation (heat rays). This makes the surrounding fuel hot enough to catch fire. The fuel burns too, first making flames and then smoking embers, until the fuel is used up.

Spreading Factors

A line of flames called a flame front moves through the forest, spreading in every direction from the source of the fire. The intensity of a fire and the speed of a flame front depend on several factors. Wind is very important. Wind brings fresh supplies of air to a fire, fanning the flames and causing a fire to burn more quickly. Wind also affects the direction in which a fire burns. A flame front moves more quickly in the direction of the wind and more slowly against the wind. Slope affects a fire, too. Fire spreads more quickly uphill because heat from a fire rises into the vegetation farther up the slope.

Fires spread across forested mountain slopes in Piva National Park, Montenegro.

In this grassland fire, the fuel is dry grass. The grass burns quickly, allowing the fire to spread rapidly to the trees.

DID YOU KNOW? When the wind conditions are right, fires can travel as fast as 22 kph (14 mph).

Forest Fire Fuel

The material that burns in a forest fire is known as fuel. A forest can contain just a couple of types of fuel or dozens of different fuels. Small trees, shrubs, and grasses on the forest floor also burn, as do fallen leaves and needles (known as litter) and fallen branches. Even rotting leaves and logs beneath the forest floor burn, and so do roots under the ground.

A firefighting plane releases its load of water as it tries to extinguish a fire.

The fire spreads quickly up mountain slopes, fanned by high winds.

CASE STUDY: CAMP FIRE CALIFORNIA USA, 2018

In November 2018, a fire started in Butte County, California, USA. Strong winds carried burning material downwind, helping the fire spread. Roads were closed and towns were evacuated. It took more than two weeks for emergency workers to contain the blaze, which burned 620 sq km² (240 mi²). In this disaster, 85 people lost their lives and nearly 19,000 structures were destroyed.

Types of Forest Fires

Firefighters classify fires by the way they spread through a forest. They divide the forest horizontally into three layers. The crown is the top layer, made up of the branches, needles, and leaves of mature trees. The surface layer is the forest floor. The ground layer is under the surface.

In 2021, wildfires raged through Greece during a summer heatwave. Smoke from the blaze clouded the skies above the capital city, Athens.

Crown, Surface, and Ground Fires

Crown fires burn in the crown. They spread through the treetops, with flames leaping from one tree to the next. They tend to occur during strong winds and spread quickly, leaving the forest floor below untouched. Crown fires happen in thick conifer forests and are the fiercest forest fires.

Surface fires burn on the forest floor, through young trees, shrubs, and grasses. They also burn fresh, dry litter that has fallen from the trees, dead logs and branches.

Ground fires burn material in the ground, under the surface. They do not burn with flames, but glow, making little smoke. They burn slowly through decaying needles and leaves, and the roots of plants, often unseen.

Surface fires normally leave the crown above untouched.

56

Kangaroos, koalas, and many other native Australian animals were killed and injured in the 2019–2020 bush fires.

In the summer of 2021, drought and high winds spread wildfires in many countries, including Turkey, Armenia, and Italy.

CASE STUDY: AUSTRALIAN BUSH FIRES, 2019–2020

Southeast Australia is one of the world's forest fire hotspots. The summers are hot and dry, and there is little rain in winter. The forests contain many eucalyptus trees, which burn easily. From June 2019 to March 2020, Australia experienced its worst wildfire season in recorded history. The fires burned through 126,000 km² (78,292 mi²) of land, 33 people lost their lives, and it is thought that around a billion animals were killed. Although Australia is used to bush fires, these were bigger, hotter, and more intense than ever before.

Fires and the Landscape

How a fire affects the forest trees depends on the type of fire and the trees themselves. A surface fire kills young trees with branches and leaves close to the ground. Older, taller trees, with bare lower trunks and crowns high up, normally survive surface fires because their thick bark protects the delicate cambium (growing layer) underneath.

Changes to Soil

Intense heat destroys some of the nutrients in forest soil. If the layer of decaying vegetation is burned, the microorganisms that recycle nutrients are also killed. On the positive side, ash from the burned plants mixes with the soil, and this ash contains nutrients such as potassium, magnesium, and calcium. Where plant roots are killed and decaying vegetation is burned, the soil has nothing to protect it from erosion. Heavy rain washes it away easily, especially on sloping ground. This leaves no soil for new plants to grow in.

Animals' instincts help them cope when a wildfire starts.

Effects on Animals

Many large animals are able to survive forest fires by running, and birds can fly away. Animals that live in underground burrows, such as rodents, survive because the soil protects them from the heat, but they may still be harmed by the heat from ground fires. However, many small animals, such as insects, cannot escape. Larger animals that do die are killed by smoke rather than flames. Animal habitats are also destroyed by fire, as are nests and eggs.

In the summer of 1988, a series of fires devastated parts of Yellowstone National Park in the northwestern United States. The intensity of the fires was caused by a lack of rain and snow over previous months. Hundreds of fires were set off by lightning. Forest officials allowed some of the fires to burn, but the fires quickly grew out of control. Over the summer months, 3,200 sq km² (1,236 mi²) of forest were burned.

The charred remains of a forest after a fire. Every tree has been damaged by the intense heat, but some trees may still be alive.

Ground fires can kill young and old trees by damaging their roots.

Even slight bark damage can let in harmful diseases and insects.

DID YOU KNOW? The fire lily flower blooms after the smoke from a wildfire has passed.

Forest Recovery

The blackened, smoldering landscape left behind by a forest fire appears lifeless. It is hard to believe that any plant or animal could live there again. But no matter how devastating a fire is, the forest always recovers eventually. A few months after the fire, green shoots begin to rise from the soil. Plants and animals gradually return, and within ten to 20 years, all but the mature trees will have returned.

Forest fires have been raging on Earth for millions of years, and forests have always recovered naturally.

Weeds to Trees

Ash from the fire supplies nutrients to plants, so growth is often rapid. Small plants such as weeds and grasses return first. These are known as pioneer plants. Some grow from seeds left in the soil. Others spread from the surrounding, unburned forest. Next come shrubs, and then trees. Plants that survive the fire also begin to grow again. Light-loving plants often thrive until the recovering trees begin to block out the light again. Animals that live on the newly growing plants return to the forest before predatory animals do.

Burned treetops let light reach the forest floor, allowing new plants to grow.

CASE STUDY:

AMAZON RAIN FOREST, 2019–2020

Unlike other forested areas of the world, not all of the Amazon rain forest is adapted to forest fires. The climate is usually too wet for fires to start naturally. However, as the Earth's climate changes, droughts are more common. Around the forest, farmers use slash–and–burn methods to clear land. Trees are cut down, and the material is burned to make space for growing crops and raising animals. In 2019 and 2020, these fires spread to the forest and blazed out of control. The Amazon rain forest is an area of high biodiversity and stores a huge amount of carbon. Areas cleared by fire can recover, but it takes a long time.

DID YOU KNOW? The seeds of a eucalyptus tree are sealed with resin, and they can open only after a fire has melted the resin.

Adapting to Fire

Some plants are well adapted to survive the heat of forest fires. For example, the giant sequoia has tough, thick bark, deep roots, and branches that are out of reach of surface fires. The aspen can grow new shoots from any of its roots that remain undamaged.

Grasses grow on the forest floor after a fire. Many trees are still charred from the flames.

Forest Fires and People

Forest fires are a serious danger to people. Although smoke gives plenty of warning of approaching flames, and most fires can be outrun, forest workers, campers, and walkers are regularly killed in forest fires. They often become confused in the smoke, heat, and noise and get trapped between two flame fronts.

Building Damage

Thousands of homes and even whole towns are built close to forests that are prone to fires. When a fire occurs, houses and other buildings are ignited by the heat from nearby burning trees, or by flying embers landing on them. Many houses in these areas are built from wood, and so they burn very quickly. The local infrastructure is also often affected. Roads and train lines are closed due to falling trees and smoke. Communication and power lines are damaged and have to be repaired.

In December 2021, a fire swept through two towns in Colorado, USA. It crossed the land quickly, reaching built-up suburbs.

Economic Damage

Timber companies plant millions of conifer trees in vast plantations, mostly in countries in the northern hemisphere. The wood from the fully grown trees is used for construction and as a source of wood pulp for papermaking. Fires are common in these plantations, particularly during hot, dry summers. Fire spreads through the densely packed trees quickly. Fire damage to plantations is extremely costly.

The smoke from forest fires can create smog in cities and affect people's health.

The Marshall prairie fire burned for 6 hours and destroyed 1,100 houses and businesses.

A forest fire threatens a house in Halkidiki, Greece. The house is at great risk because it is surrounded by trees.

CASE STUDY: PORTUGAL, 2017

In 2017, terrible wildfires broke out in Portugal in June and October. Much of the country is covered in forest, and winds sweep across it from the Atlantic Ocean. Portugal has vast forests of eucalyptus trees, which burn very easily. Many believe that forests were not managed well, making fires too hard to tackle when they did break out. Roads were blocked by the fire, trapping people so that they could not escape. It is thought that around 120 people died in the two episodes, and many more were injured. Houses and businesses were destroyed, and many regions took years to rebuild.

DID YOU KNOW? In the state of Oregon, USA, in 2020, 5,000 km² (1,930 mi²) were burned and more than 3,000 homes.

Fighting Forest Fires

The first stage in fighting a forest fire is to detect that the fire has started. If this is done early, the fire can be stopped before it grows. If a fire has become established, firefighters use information about the fuel in the forest, the weather, and the terrain to decide how to tackle the fire.

Fire Detection

At times of high fire risk, people are always on the lookout for telltale smoke from forest fires. In some places, there are manned fire-watch stations on hilltops. In others, rangers patrol the forest in vehicles or in aircraft. If smoke is spotted, the next step is to pinpoint the exact location of the fire. This is not easy in cases where there is lots of smoke, so an aircraft carrying a heat-sensing infrared scanner flies over the area. Once the fire has been pinpointed, maps can be drawn for the fire control team. Now, firefighters move into position by foot, truck, and aircraft.

Many people were evacuated from their homes as wildfires spread across Greece in August 2021. Hundreds of firefighters tackled the blaze.

SMOKE JUMPERS

In very remote areas, it would take many hours for trucks to reach a fire. So the initial attack on the fire is made by firefighters called smoke jumpers (or fire jumpers). They parachute into the forest carrying all the equipment they need, plus food, water, and first-aid equipment. Smoke jumpers can often reach a fire in its early stages, before it has a chance to spread.

DID YOU KNOW? During the Australian bush fires in 2019–20, flames reached 100 m (328 ft) high.

A firefighting plane releases its load of water as it tries to extinguish a fire in Greece.

Direct and Indirect Attack

Firefighters attack a fire directly or indirectly, or sometimes with both methods. Direct firefighting is used on small fires before they spread. Firefighters try to put the fire out by hosing it with water, covering it with earth or ash, raking away the fuel, or hitting it with beaters. Indirect firefighting is used on intense fires. Firefighters do not try to put out the flames, but they try to keep the fire from spreading. They clear sections of forest ahead of the flame front, creating firebreaks that the fire cannot cross. They light fires called backfires that burn toward the flame front, using up the fuel.

What Are Volcanoes?

A volcano is a hill, mountain, or rift in the ground where molten rock, called magma, erupts to the surface from deep under the ground. Above ground, the magma is known as lava. The ground around a volcano has lava that has cooled and solidified, together with cinders and ash. The red-hot rivers of lava, towering clouds of ash, and thick flows of mud of an eruption devastate the landscape.

Volcano Fuego in Guatemala is one of the most active in South America. Most of its eruptions are small.

Volcanoes and the Landscape

Much of Earth's surface is made up of rocks that have come from volcanoes. Volcanoes create and build mountains and islands, but they can also be destructive. They cover the landscape with lava, ash, and mud, burning and burying plants and destroying animal habitats. Houses, villages, and towns may also be buried or burned, and thousands of people may be killed or injured.

Vulcan's Island

The word *volcano* comes from Vulcano, an island off the coast of Italy. The ancient Romans believed that the god Vulcan lived in a volcano on the island, where he made weapons—such as arrows and lightning bolts—for the other gods. Fiery eruptions from the island's volcanoes were believed to be sparks from Vulcan's forge.

CASE STUDY: KRAKATAU, 1883

One of the biggest volcanic eruptions ever recorded happened in 1883. A volcano on the tiny island of Krakatau in Indonesia erupted with a series of enormous explosions. The explosions were so loud, they could be heard more than 4,800 km (3,000 mi) away. The island itself was blasted to pieces, leaving a massive crater. Hot ash clouds destroyed villages 50 km (30 mi) away across the sea, and giant waves swamped nearby coasts, killing more than 36,400 people.

Molten rock from beneath Earth's crust bursts out of a volcano.

Volcanoes have been erupting since Earth formed 4.5 billion years ago.

DID YOU KNOW? A new volcano named Anak Krakatau (child of Krakatau) is growing where Krakatau erupted.

How Do Volcanoes Form?

The boundary of Eurasian and North American tectonic plates runs through Iceland. The island was formed as the two plates pulled apart and is part of the Mid-Atlantic Ridge.

Volcanoes form in places where molten rock forces its way upward through a crack in Earth's surface. The molten rock, or magma, comes from deep underground from a layer of Earth called the mantle. The mantle lies beneath the solid upper layer of Earth, called the crust (see page 8).

Moving Plates

Earth's crust is cracked into huge pieces called tectonic plates. The plates drift on the hot rock beneath, but most move less than 3 cm (1 inch) per year. Scientists think they are moved by slow, swirling currents in the mantle. Most volcanoes form where two plates meet. The lines between plates are called plate boundaries or faults.

At some faults, two plates collide, and one plate is pushed under the other and into the mantle. These faults are called destructive faults or subduction zones. The plate that is pushed down melts, making magma that rises again to produce volcanoes.

Iceland is on a boundary between two tectonic plates that are moving away from each other. The rocks here are being torn apart, making giant cracks in the landscape.

DID YOU KNOW? Iceland has 130 volcanoes!

Submerged Volcanoes

At some boundaries, two plates move apart. These are called divergent or constructive faults. Magma rises up to fill the gap between the plates. As it cools, it forms new crust. Beneath the oceans, many volcanoes have formed at constructive faults. The Mid-Atlantic Ridge is a slow-spreading ridge under the Atlantic Ocean. It extends for around 16,000 km (10,000 mi). Mountains formed by the ridge are so tall that their tops reach above sea level, forming islands such as the Azores.

Many volcanoes have formed on Iceland. In 2021, the Fagradalsfjall volcano erupted after 800 years of silence.

The Hawaiian island chain has formed over a hotspot under the Pacific Ocean plate. There are 132 islands stretching more than 2,400 km (1,500 mi).

HOTSPOT VOLCANOES

Some volcanoes grow in the middle of tectonic plates, far from where plates are colliding or spreading apart. Scientists think that they form over "hotspots" in the mantle where magma forces it way up through the crust. Hotspot volcanoes in the middle of oceans form undersea mountains called seamounts. The islands of Hawaii in the middle of the Pacific Ocean are the summits of giant seamounts.

Inside a Volcano

At the top of a volcano, there is often a dish-shaped hollow called a caldera. Beneath the crater, a vent stretches down into Earth's crust. At the bottom of the vent, there is a chamber full of magma. As more magma collects in the chamber, pressure builds until an eruption results. During an eruption, magma rises through the vent and out into the air.

Sugarloaf Mountain in Rio de Janeiro, Brazil, is made of magma that solidified in the vent of a volcano.

A Composite Cone

Most volcanoes on land, such as Mount Fuji in Japan and Vesuvius in Italy, are tall cones made up of layers of lava and ash. The layers are formed by many eruptions over hundreds, thousands, or millions of years. There is a central main vent and side vents that lead to the volcano's lower slopes. This type of volcano is called a composite cone or stratovolcano. It is like a giant heap of loose rubble. Magma sometimes flows in between the layers of lava and ash and then solidifies, making the volcano more stable.

Mount Vesuvius in Italy is a stratovolcano.

ACTIVE, DORMANT, AND EXTINCT

Scientists classify volcanoes as active, dormant, or extinct. An active volcano is known to have erupted in the last 10,000 years. There are about 500 active volcanoes in the world. A dormant volcano is an active volcano that is not erupting at the moment. An extinct volcano is a volcano that nobody has ever seen erupt and is not expected to erupt again—although that does not mean it never will!

The volcano's cone has been eroded away over thousands of years.

In a composite cone or stratovolcano, magma rises up the vent from the magma chamber. The volcano's layers consist of material from previous eruptions.

Magma Ingredients

Magma is molten rock. Some types of magma are runny and flow easily, like syrup. Others are thick and sticky, like tar. Magma also contains gas dissolved in it. When magma is deep inside Earth, high pressure keeps the gas dissolved. When the magma rises up through the vent of a volcano, the gas is released and bursts out of the volcano with the molten rock.

DID YOU KNOW? The hottest magma can reach 1,200°C (2,192°F).

Shields and Cinders

Not all volcanic eruptions are the same. While gentle eruptions produce rivers of red-hot lava, violent eruptions produce towering clouds of ash but very little lava. Other eruptions produce both ash and lava. These different types of eruption build different types of volcano.

Shield Volcanoes

Shield volcanoes are made by gentle eruptions. They happen at constructive faults and at hotspots, where thin, runny lava comes up from the ground. A shield volcano is wide and low with gently sloping sides, like an upside-down plate. During an eruption, gas in the magma makes it shoot upwards, firing blobs of lava out of the vent in spectacular fountains. The lava falls to the ground and flows down the volcano's sides in glowing rivers called lava flows. Gradually, the lava cools and turns to solid rock. Over thousands or millions of years, the lava flows build on top of each other to make a mountain.

A shield volcano in the western highlands near Thingvellir, Iceland.

Cinder Cones

Sometimes the gas in magma forms bubbles in the blobs of lava that hurtle out of a volcano. The blobs cool in the air and fall to the ground as red or black pieces of rock called cinders. The cinders pile up to form a steep-sided volcano called a cinder cone. Cinder cones often form on the sides of shield volcanoes.

Haleakala volcano, on the island of Maui, Hawaii, is a dormant volcano that rises all the way from the seabed.

The cinder cones that formed from magma when the volcano erupted have created a bright landscape.

HAWAIIAN ERUPTIONS

Eruptions that produce lava fountains and lava flows are called Hawaiian eruptions because they happen regularly on the island of Hawaii in the Pacific Ocean. Hawaii is made up of five giant shield volcanoes. One of them, Kilauea, is the most active volcano on Earth. Past eruptions were more violent than they are today. Kilauea erupted almost continuously between 1983 and 2018 and began again in 2020.

DID YOU KNOW? January has been chosen as Hawaii's Volcano Awareness Month.

Explosive Volcanoes

A towering cloud of ash is called an eruption column. The biggest eruptions produce columns more than 50 km (30 mi) high.

Volcanoes at destructive faults erupt violently. The eruptions are dramatic and dangerous, and have created some of the greatest explosions in Earth's history. They happen because the magma at destructive boundaries is thick and sticky. It blocks a volcano's vent until the pressure from the magma chamber underneath builds up so much that the magma is forced upward.

Plinian Eruptions

Sometimes the gas in magma cannot bubble upwards because the magma is too thick. Instead it explodes, blasting the molten rock into tiny pieces. These violent eruptions build steep-sided volcanoes made up of layers of ash and lava called composite cones or stratovolcanoes. During a Plinian eruption, a high-speed jet of hot gas fires tiny pieces of molten rock into the air. These pieces are smaller than grains of sand but quickly solidify to form clouds of ash. The gas jet eventually slows down, but the hot gases continue to float upward through the atmosphere, carrying the ash with them.

The effects of a volcano's enormous heat can be seen in this house on the island of Java, Indonesia, following the eruption of Merapi Volcano.

Volcanic Hurricanes

Ash clouds are often so thick with ash and small drops of molten rock that they cannot keep rising into the air. Instead, they collapse and surge down the sides of a volcano. These billowing, red-hot ash and gas avalanches are called pyroclastic flows or volcanic hurricanes.

DID YOU KNOW? Pyroclastic flows typically travel at over 80 kph (50 mph).

Pyroclastic flows spread quickly from the volcano and can even travel over water!

Today, the crater of Mount Pinatubo is peaceful.

CASE STUDY: MOUNT PINATUBO, 1991

The eruption of Mount Pinatubo in the Philippines in 1991 was the second-largest of the 20th century. Pinatubo had not erupted for 400 years. The eruption began with rumbling noises from the mountain. It ended with a series of massive explosions that blew 260 m (850 ft) off the top of the mountain and formed an ash cloud 35 km (22 mi) high, turning the sky black for weeks. The cloud spread all the way around the world.

Mountains and Islands

Volcanoes start life as vents in the ground. As soon as they start erupting, a hill begins to form from the ash, lava, or cinders that are ejected from them. Eventually, the hill may become a volcano reaching high above the landscape.

Astronomical Observatories on Mauna Kea mountain peak on Big Island of Hawaii.

Volcanic Islands

Lava that erupts on the seafloor piles up into undersea mountains called seamounts. If the volcano keeps on erupting, it eventually forms a new island. Volcanic islands grow along destructive faults. They form long, curving chains of islands called island arcs. Volcanic islands also form over hotspots and sometimes over spreading ridges. Mauna Kea on the island of Hawaii is the tip of a seamount that rises 10,211 m (33, 407 ft) from the seabed, making it the tallest mountain on Earth.

Volcanic Rocks

When volcanic rock cools and solidifies, it forms igneous rock. There are many different types of igneous rocks. Runny lava from shield volcanoes cools to make a black rock called basalt. The part of Earth's crust that forms the seabed is made from basalt. Volcanic ash that falls from clouds and pyroclastic flows builds up in thick layers. Gradually, the bottom layers are squeezed together and turn into a rock called tuff.

Na Pali Coast mountain landscape in Kauai island, Hawaii, USA.

In February 1943, a Mexican farmer named Dionisio Pulido began to feel small earthquakes and noticed that the ground under his feet was warm. Soon, a crack opened in his fields, and ash and lava began to pour out. A volcano began erupting in front of his eyes! By July, the volcano was 300 m (1,000 ft) high, and Dionisio's village had been buried. When the eruption eventually stopped in 1952, the cone had reached 424 m (1,391 ft). The volcano is named Paricutín.

Volcanoes can be single mountains, such as Mount Fuji in Japan, or part of huge mountain ranges, such as the Andes in South America.

The cone of Mount Fuji in Japan rises to 3,776 m (12,389 ft). Mount Fuji last erupted in 1707.

DID YOU KNOW? The Mexican volcano Paricutín is one of Earth's youngest volcanoes.

77

Blown Apart

Volcanic eruptions build up volcanoes and make new rock, but the eruptions of composite cone volcanoes are also very destructive. They blow volcanoes to pieces and create vast holes in Earth's surface.

Blowing Its Top

The eruption of a large volcano can be so violent that it blows the top off the volcano, leaving the volcano lower than before. This happens when thick magma has built up inside the vent but cannot get out. Ash and rock are blown into the air and also cascade down the mountainside.

Composite volcanoes eventually become unstable. Pressure from the magma inside makes their upper slopes bulge and collapse, sending down avalanches of ash and rock that spread out from the volcano. This releases the magma, which explodes sideways out of the volcano.

Crater Lake in Oregon, USA, lies in a caldera formed when Mount Mazama collapsed in a volcanic eruption 7,700 years ago. The cone-shaped island is a sign that volcanic activity is continuing.

Calderas

A caldera is a giant volcanic crater. A caldera forms when explosive eruptions leave an empty space in a volcano's magma chamber, and the ground above collapses into the chamber. The largest calderas are more than 50 km (30 mi) across and were formed by gigantic eruptions in the distant past. Three of the largest calderas on Earth are in Yellowstone National Park in the United States. The longest is 80 km (50 mi) long. They were formed by the eruption and collapse of incredibly large volcanoes more than 500,000 years ago.

DID YOU KNOW? The Yellowstone eruptions were a thousand times more powerful than the eruption of Mount St. Helens and buried half of North America under ash.

The ash plume from the 1980 Mount St. Helens eruption lasted for 9 hours. Forests, roads, bridges, and buildings were destroyed by volcanic mudflows called lahars.

A series of earthquakes and small explosions led up to the eruption of Mount St. Helens.

CASE STUDY: MOUNT ST. HELENS, 1980

The top of Mount St. Helens in Washington state in the northwestern United States was blown apart by an eruption in 1980. The eruption began with small earthquakes caused by magma moving underground. Ash clouds rose from the crater. Then the north face of the mountain began to bulge outward. Eventually, the bulge collapsed and slid downward in a massive avalanche. The collapse released magma that exploded, blowing 400 m (1,300 ft) of the mountain top to pieces and leaving a gaping hole.

Environmental Effects

The lava, ash, and gas from a volcanic eruption can affect the countryside all around a volcano. Lava flows spread across the landscape, covering it, and burning and burying trees and fields. Most lava flows are slow moving and travel only a short way before they cool and stop. But ash clouds and pyroclastic flows from violent eruptions are much more dangerous.

Ash Layers

Violent eruptions from volcanoes throw vast clouds of ash into the atmosphere. Winds can carry the clouds, leaving a dusting of ash on the ground far away from the eruption. Deep ash deposits make it impossible for plants to grow, turning green countryside into a dusty desert. Pyroclastic flows have the most devastating effects. They sweep downhill, scorching the ground with hot gas, ash, and rocks as they go. Trees are knocked down and burned, and animals are killed instantly.

Molten lava flows into the Pacific Ocean from the Big Island of Hawaii. The island's landscape is formed by its volcanoes.

Eruption of the volcano Puyehue, Chile

Global Effects

Ash from the biggest eruptions travels high into the atmosphere. It stays there for weeks or months and is carried by winds. This ash blocks sunlight, which can make the weather slightly colder all over the world.

In 1815, a volcano named Tambora erupted on the Indonesian island of Sumbawa. Scientists think that this was the biggest eruption in the last 10,000 years. It threw 30 times as much ash into the atmosphere as Mount St. Helens in 1980. The ash spread around the world, blocking out the sun. This caused cold, damp weather in many places over many months. Crops could not grow properly, and there were food shortages that caused riots. In some places, 1816 was nicknamed "the year without summer."

A satellite image shows a plume of ash blowing away from Mount Etna on the island of Sicily in Italy. Winds can carry ash around the world.

When gases from volcanic eruptions mix with rain, it can create acid rain, which damages plants and wildlife.

DID YOU KNOW? The eruption of Tambora led to the invention of the bicycle, because there were fewer horses for people to ride on!

Mud and Flood

The landscape around volcanoes is not just affected by lava, ash clouds, and pyroclastic flows. Water also causes problems. Water from melting glaciers mixes with ash and pours down the sides of volcanoes in mudflows. Water released in eruptions causes floods, and explosive volcanoes cause giant waves at sea.

In 1995, a volcanic area in the Soufriere Hills, on the southern part of the Caribbean island of Monserrat, began to be active after 300 years of being dormant. The eruptions went on for five years.

Mudflows

Giant composite cone volcanoes are high, and their summits are covered in snow and ice all year round. During an eruption, the heat from the magma melts the snow and ice to make water. The water flows down the volcano's slopes, mixing with ash to form thick mudflows. These flows are called lahars. The mud hurtles along river valleys at speeds of over 200 kph (120 mph) downhill, destroying everything in its path. It can flow up to 300 km (186 mi) before coming to a stop. Then the mud sets hard, like concrete. Mudflows also happen when heavy rain mixes with fresh falls of ash. The rain often comes from thunderstorms that happen inside ash clouds.

CASE STUDY: ICELAND FLOOD, 1996

Part of Iceland is covered in a thick sheet of ice called an ice cap. Underneath the ice cap are several volcanoes. Occasionally, the erupting volcanoes melt the ice, causing floods that flow down to the sea. An eruption in 1996 caused water to gather under the ice cap for days before suddenly breaking out in a colossal flood. The flood carried chunks of ice the size of houses for 15 km (9.3 mi), covering the land between the ice cap and the sea with ash and rock.

Volcanic eruptions on Monserrat were most explosive in 1997. Most people were evacuated to the north and nearby islands. Plymouth, the capital city, was covered in ash and mud from lahars.

Evidence has been found of a massive tsunami wave caused when the volcanic island now called Santorini in Greece erupted around 1600 BCE.

DID YOU KNOW? Volcanoes at sea can cause giant waves called tsunamis.

Living with Volcanoes

About half a billion people, or one in 16 of the world's population, live in places that are at risk from volcanoes. Their homes could be hit by lava flows, pyroclastic flows, or mudflows. Many live on old lava flows and in valleys that have been swept by mudflows or pyroclastic flows in the past.

Volcanic Soil

Millions of people live near volcanoes because there is nowhere else for them to live. Others choose to take a risk because volcanoes produce fertile soil and are good places to farm. The soil on the lower slopes of volcanoes is made from eroded lava and ash. It is full of minerals that plants need to grow, which makes it excellent for growing crops. Many huge coffee plantations are located on volcanoes in Central America, for example, and there are many vineyards around Mount Vesuvius. Farmers often return to volcanic slopes even after their farms have been destroyed by eruptions, because the soil is so rich.

There are other advantages to living near volcanoes. Volcanic rocks make good building materials. Lava and tuff can be sawn into building blocks, and cinders are used on the surface of paths and roads. The heat from hot rocks in volcanic areas is used to heat water and to generate electricity.

Naples in Italy could be affected by pyroclastic flows from a major eruption of Vesuvius.

DID YOU KNOW? When Mount Vesuvius erupted in 79 CE the towns of Pompeii and Herculaneum were covered with volcanic ash and debris.

Vesuvius was most recently active from 1913 to 1944. Today, it is carefully monitored. The area surrounding it is now a National Park, and you can walk to the crater.

When Mayon volcano shows signs of activity, people are evacuated from the surrounding towns and villages.

CASE STUDY: FARMING ON MAYON

The Mayon volcano in the Philippines is one of Earth's most active volcanoes. It has both low level eruptions and more serious events. Farmers use the lower slopes to grow crops, but it is a risky way to live. Mayon has erupted more than 40 times since records began in 1616. The worst eruption was in 1814 when 1,200 were killed. An eruption in 1993 caused 79 deaths. It erupted again in 2000, 2006, 2009, 2013, and 2018. Scientists monitor the volcano's activity closely so that people can be warned of danger.

What Is a Tsunami?

The Great Japan earthquake in 2011 caused a series of tsunamis to flood the coastal regions.

A tsunami is a huge wave that can flood the land with devastating effects. When a tsunami hits a waterfront or other shore area used by people, its destructive power is felt. It can flood towns and villages with little warning, destroying all in its path and killing people and animals. When the wave retreats, everything can be swept out to sea.

Tsunamis through Time

There have probably been tsunamis for as long as there has been sea. One of the earliest descriptions was left by the Greek historian Thucydides, who described a tsunami in the Mediterranean Sea near Greece in 426 BCE: "The sea … returned in a huge wave and invaded a great part of the town, and retreated, leaving some of it still underwater; so that what was once land is now sea; such of the inhabitants perishing as could not run up to the higher ground in time." Thucydides linked the tsunami to recent earthquakes in the area—modern scientists would do the same.

CASE STUDY: WHEN THE SEA AND SKY FELL

Modern geologists point to evidence of a tsunami caused by a meteorite striking the Tasman Sea between 500 and 850 years ago. This may explain a legend told by the people of Burragorang in Australia. One night, just after sunset, the sky shuddered, heaved, and tumbled, crashing down on them. The Milky Way split, and stars fell—including a gigantic, burning blue star that tore the ground apart, showering the people with chunks of earth and rock. Later, other tribes told of the whole ocean falling on them from above. It then rained for weeks, and the whole land was flooded. The native peoples believed that these events were caused by an angry ancestor in the sky.

What Causes Tsunamis?

Tsunamis are caused by a disturbance in or under the sea that makes a large volume of water move suddenly. Most are caused by earthquakes—though landslides, volcanic eruptions, and even meteorites falling into the sea can cause tsunamis.

As the wave retreated, debris and people were pulled along with the force of the water. Low-lying areas were left flooded.

"The Great Wave off Kanagawa", by Katsushika Hokusai, was painted in the early nineteenth Century.

The Tsunami Zone

Tsunamis can happen anywhere, but most occur around the Pacific Ocean. Volcanic eruptions and earthquakes are very common around the edges of the Pacific, both inland and just off the coast, and these can trigger tsunamis that spread across the whole ocean.

Inland Tsunamis

Tsunamis can even happen in an inland sea or lake. There have been many tsunamis in the Mediterranean Sea, which is largely enclosed by Europe and North Africa. Earthquakes and volcanic activity around Italy and Greece have caused some disastrous tsunamis throughout history, including some believed to have destroyed ancient Greek and Minoan cities thousands of years ago.

Landfall

A tsunami can strike land a long way from the event that causes it—even on the other side of the ocean. In 1946, a tsunami that struck the Hawaiian Islands in the middle of the Pacific Ocean was caused by an earthquake in the Aleutian Trench, off the coast of Alaska, five hours earlier. The earthquake was over 4,000 km (2,485 mi) from Hawaii. When a tsunami reaches the shore quickly, near to the source of the earthquake or eruption, it brings new devastation to an area hit only minutes before.

In places where tsunamis may happen, warning signs are put up to alert people of the danger.

DID YOU KNOW? Lakes and rivers can also be affected by tsunamis. In 1812, New Madrid, Missouri, USA, was struck by a large earthquake, and the flow of the Mississippi River was temporarily reversed.

Off the southern coast of Alaska, the Pacific and North American plates
meet at the Fairweather Fault system. Here, the plates move horizontally
past each other at around 50 mm (2 in) per year. In 1958, the fault
system caused an earthquake that caused a huge landslide at the head
of Lituya Bay. The landslide crashed into the water, sending huge waves
through the bay. One wave reached 500 m (1700 ft) high on land.

In 2011, an
earthquake off
the coast of
Japan caused
an enormous
tsunami.

The tsunami caused
devastation as waves
up to 10 m (33 ft)
high struck the land.
The disaster is known
as the Great East
Japan Earthquake.

Earthquakes and Tsunamis

An earthquake is caused by the violent movement of Earth's tectonic plates. When a plate moves underneath the ocean, a vast quantity of water is displaced and huge waves are sent rushing across the ocean.

The 2004 Indian Ocean tsunami affected 13 countries. Indonesia was the worst hit.

Moving Plates

Tsunamis are usually caused by big earthquakes—ones that measure 7.6 or above. Tectonic plates that move suddenly downward, are most likely to set off a tsunami, but they can also be caused by horizontal movement. Landslides and avalanches caused by earthquakes can also trigger tsunamis as huge amounts of rock slip into the water.

Filling the Gap

When Earth's crust under the sea suddenly slips, a massive column of water may fall quickly downward, rushing in to fill a gap, or it may be rapidly thrust upward. Under gravity, the water immediately evens out, correcting itself to regain a smooth surface. As it does so, a series of massive waves is thrown out. If there is an earthquake on land, ripples of energy, just like waves on water but moving more slowly, run through the solid ground. If they meet the sea, the ripples are transferred to waves in the water.

A tsunami is a series of huge waves. It washes against the coast several times with great speed and force.

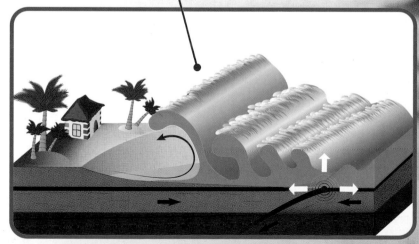

DID YOU KNOW? More than 80% of the tsunamis in the Pacific over the last 2,000 years have been caused by earthquakes.

CASE STUDY: LISBON, 1755

In November 1755, Lisbon in Portugal was rocked by one of the most powerful earthquakes in recorded history. Lasting ten minutes, it measured 9.0 on the Richter scale (a scale for measuring earthquake intensity) and demolished much of the city. People fled to the beach to escape falling buildings, but when a huge tsunami struck minutes later, many were killed. The tsunami possibly reached as far as Brazil in South America. A third of the population of Lisbon died—more than 100,000 people in total. Modern earthquake research began with this disaster.

Volcanoes and Tsunamis

The very same areas that are plagued by earthquakes also suffer volcanic eruptions. As the oceanic crust is forced downward, it melts underground. Some rises through the Earth's upper layer to swell vast magma chambers beneath volcanoes. When a volcano can hold no more, the magma is hurled out under pressure, making an eruption.

Water and Fire

If a volcano is on the coast, or is an island in the sea, water and molten rock make an explosive mixture. Water rushing into the magma chamber often causes an explosion so violent that the volcano is blown apart, and the sudden movement of a large volume of water can cause a tsunami. Many volcanoes are completely underwater. An undersea eruption can force a column of water upward, or the seafloor can collapse into an emptying magma chamber. Either event can cause a tsunami.

Anak Krakatau has had frequent eruptions since 1927.

CASE STUDY: ANAK KRAKATAU, 2018

Following the 1883 eruption of Krakatau, volcanic activity created a new cone inside the caldera. This cone is called Anak Krakatau, or "Child of Krakatau." In December 2018, it erupted, causing a tsunami of more than 80 m (260 ft) and causing nearly 500 deaths. Anak Krakatau erupted again in 2020 and continues to be active.

DID YOU KNOW? Earth tremors can be the first sign that a volcano is about to erupt. Either the earth tremors or the eruption itself can cause a tsunami.

When Anak Krakatau erupted in 2018, a large part of the volcano collapsed, which caused a huge tsunami.

Watery Buildup

A tsunami may start far out at sea or near the coast. In the area of the Ring of Fire, there are often volcanic eruptions and earthquakes near the coast. An earthquake under the water makes a series of waves that travel outward in a circle from the epicenter (starting point) of the quake.

Near and Far

On the side nearest the shore, the waves reach land quickly—often before there has been time to warn people living in the area. The wave that strikes the coast nearby is called a local tsunami. But waves travel outward in all directions, and some travel huge distances, crossing the ocean to hit land on the other side—a distant tsunami.

The city of Palu, Central Sulawesi, sits at the end of a long, narrow bay. When an earthquake triggered a tsunami in 2018, the city was left in ruins.

Starting Small

Far out at sea, the tsunami is a tiny wave, but it can travel as fast as a commercial jet—over 750 kph (466 mph). The height of the wave may be only 60 cm (24 in), and so it often goes unnoticed by ships in the area. As the tsunami approaches land and the water gets shallower, the wave slows down and grows much taller. By the time it reaches the shore, it can be 30 m (98 ft) tall or even taller and slow to 50 kph (31 mph).

Very high wave on the shore

Small wave in the ocean

Remains constant

Upward wave

Earthquake

DID YOU KNOW? Although the word *tsunami* is spelled with a t, it is pronounced "soo-NAH-mee."

In September 2018, an earthquake close to the city of Palu, Central Sulawesi, sent tsunami waves as high as 11 m (36 ft) rushing on shore. The tsunami was larger than expected for the size of the earthquake, and some scientists think that an underwater landslide might have increased the size of the tsunami. Around 4,300 lives were lost in the disaster.

As well as causing a tsunami, the earthquake also caused the ground to become soft and building foundations to become unstable.

Minute by Minute

A tsunami can bring total devastation in just a few terrifying minutes. The most destructive tsunamis are those that strike without warning, because it takes most people only about ten minutes to move to safety if they know a tsunami is on its way.

Flooding

A tsunami is rarely a big breaking wave. Instead, the sea level swells and rises, and a flood washes in over the land. Froth and breaking waves come from the flood hitting features of the landscape and buildings, and from water falling over walls and through windows. The way the wave behaves depends on the shape and geographical features of the coastline. If there are lots of areas of coastline exposed, with inlets and promontories, a complex pattern of flooding can occur, with water moving in several directions. Sometimes a river can funnel a wave far inland, or a dock can trap a wave so that it bounces backward and forward off the walls.

In some cases, the sea draws back before the tsunami strikes, and sometimes before it is even visible. This is the wave pulling the sea into itself. On the shore, old shipwrecks may be revealed. Fish may be stranded on the beach. People are often killed because they rush to pick up the fish. There may be a hissing and cracking sound—or a rumble like thunder—as the tsunami approaches.

This CCTV image was taken during the Great East Japan Earthquake in March 2011. Water flows over an embankment and floods the city of Miyako.

A house has been drawn out to sea by the strength of the water.

DID YOU KNOW? A wave measuring 0.3 m (1 ft) reached Antarctica 18 hours after the disaster in Japan.

Wave After Wave

Tsunamis are really a "wave train" with more waves following the first at an interval of anything from five to 90 minutes. People sometimes return to the area after the first wave, thinking that the tsunami is over. They may then be killed or swept away by the next wave, which is frequently bigger than the first.

In the disaster, around 20,000 lives were lost. Many of these deaths were a result of the tsunami.

CASE STUDY: JAPAN, 2011

In March 2011, a huge earthquake struck off Japan's east coast. A tsunami arrived 30 minutes after the earthquake. At its highest, it reached 40 m (130 ft) and affected a huge 2,000 km (1,242 mi) stretch of coastline. The tsunami damaged a nuclear power plant, destroyed 123,000 houses, and damaged a million more. Other countries were also affected by the mega-wave including Hawaii, the United States, French Polynesia, the Galapagos Islands, Peru, and Chile.

Human Catastrophe

A tsunami can wreak terrible devastation if it strikes a populated area. In some of the areas in the Pacific that are frequently hit by tsunamis, many people live by fishing and spend their whole lives on the shore, in the danger area.

Survivors can suffer terrible consequences if their homes and livelihoods are wrecked and their communities destroyed.

Death and Destruction

Drowning is not the only risk a tsunami brings. People may be thrown against hard objects by the force of the water, crushed by falling buildings, or hit by debris carried on the flood. They may be dragged out to sea as the tsunami recedes. When the waters drop, the danger is far from over. Disease spreads quickly in hot, wet conditions. With no sanitation or clean water, and often with the dead bodies of people and animals lying unburied on land and in the water, cholera, diphtheria, typhoid, dysentery, and other deadly diseases quickly take hold and spread.

Cut Off

Often, roads, waterfronts, quays, and runways are swept away or rendered useless by flooding. They may be filled with debris, which makes it difficult for aid to reach the stricken area and for injured people to be taken to safety. There may be no drinking water, food, emergency shelter, or medical supplies for several days, especially in remote areas.

The 2018 tsunami and earthquake near Palu, Central Sulawesi, Indonesia, destroyed a main bridge.

CASE STUDY:

INDIAN OCEAN, 2004

In December 2004, an earthquake in the Indian Ocean caused the most devastating tsunami in human history. Nearly 230,000 people were killed or reported missing, most of them in Sumatra, Thailand, Sri Lanka, and India. The area was left with destroyed communities and land that could not be used, scattered with wreckage and stripped of vegetation. Waves from the tsunami were detected as far away as Antarctica and the coast of South America.

Disease can kill as many people as the tsunami itself.

DID YOU KNOW? 1.7 million people were made homeless by the 2004 Indian Ocean tsunami.

99

Sending Help

People struck by tsunamis and other natural disasters need help immediately, and for the following months or years. After the emergency services have rescued people who are trapped, injured, or drifting in the sea, the next job is to provide food, shelter, water, and medical help. After that, the work of rebuilding lives and communities must begin.

International aid can step in, with expert emergency teams, assistance from armed forces, and charity or aid workers.

Emergency Services

Police, coastguards, ambulance, and fire services may all be involved in emergency relief. They are needed to rescue people from the water, from trees and rooftops where they have taken refuge, and from under debris and inside collapsed buildings. They must also take on the difficult task of removing dead bodies. If the tsunami is large and affects a wide area, local services may not be able to cope, or they may be put out of action themselves. If some areas are cut off by water or by piles of debris, clearing routes to and within the disaster area is a crucial early stage of relief work.

Keeping in Touch

If local communication links are destroyed, radio, phones, and computers with wireless Internet links are a crucial means of keeping in touch. In the Indian Ocean tsunami of 2004, survivors, volunteer helpers, and aid workers used text messages to guide rescuers to trapped victims. They used blogs to keep the outside world updated.

International aid with expert emergency teams

Following the Indian Ocean tsunami in 2004, international emergency teams arrived quickly. The immediate aid needed in the area was water purification units, tents, medicines, food, and skilled medical staff. Money was donated by countries around the world, by individuals giving to charities, and by international organizations such as the World Bank.

Many ordinary people in the area join the rescue efforts. Even without expert knowledge, they can give crucial help in locating people and helping them to safety.

DID YOU KNOW? Japan estimated that it would take $309 billion to rebuild after the Great East Japan earthquake and tsunami in 2011.

Terrible Aftermath

The effects of a major tsunami can last years or even decades. For people who have lost family members, the effects last a lifetime. As well as the personal tragedies, the loss of communities, buildings, farmland, and forest, and changes to the coast, often cause financial disaster, adding to the trauma for survivors.

Personal Tragedies

A tsunami can kill large proportions of the local population, and many may lose a number of family members and friends. Often, people are missing, with no body ever recovered, and many bodies that are recovered are not identifiable. Orphaned children, or those separated from their parents in the chaos, must be reunited with family members. With children too small or traumatized to communicate, this can be very difficult.

Broken Communities

In some places, too few people are left alive to rebuild a community. A tsunami commonly destroys buildings, farms, fishing grounds, forest, roads, and other amenities and natural areas that are vital to people living in the area. In the aftermath, many people cannot make a living and may have no home or shelter. The devastation can have a financial impact for many years. National and international aid is used to help people rebuild homes and establish a livelihood in the wrecked environment.

An emergency school is provided inside the temporary shelter for the tsunami victims in Phang Nga, Thailand, 2005.

Banda Aceh was the closest major city to the epicenter of the earthquake that caused the 2004 tsunami.

Huge amounts of debris are left behind when tsunami floodwaters recede (go down).

CASE STUDY: PAPUA NEW GUINEA, 1998

In July 1998, a 15 m (49 ft) high tsunami swept across an area of land in Papua New Guinea with devastating results for the 10,000 inhabitants and their homes. The wave arrived without warning, following an earthquake only 30 km (18 mi) away. Many of the victims were children, who were playing near the beaches during the school holiday. The community faced a difficult future with a whole generation lost. Raymond Nimis, a survivor, described what happened: "I felt the earthquake rocking the house. It was dark. Then we heard the sea break. I saw it, very huge. We we tried to run, but it was too late".

DID YOU KNOW? In the Indian Ocean tsunami, many more women than men died, and local communities had to adapt to different social structures after the event.

Rebuilding

It can take a long time for an area to recover from a big tsunami. National and international efforts are often needed to address all the different areas of rebuilding, from cleaning up the environment to putting up new buildings, resettling communities, and providing emotional and psychological help for victims.

Following the Japanese tsunami in 2011, a survey group studied the way the tsunami spread along the coast and which areas had been worst hit.

Back to Normal

It's important for the people affected by a disaster to return to some kind of normal life as quickly as possible. Providing schools and at least temporary homes is a priority once the immediate needs for food, water, and medicines have been met. Often, there is a conflict between people wanting to build traditional homes that they can afford to build, and engineers who may advise building in different ways and places, in order to avoid future damage. It is a sensitive issue that needs careful handling. It is not just houses and businesses that are destroyed by a tsunami. Public facilities, such as schools and hospitals, must be rebuilt, roads and waterways must be repaired, and vital utilities such as water, electricity, and communications networks must all be restored before normal life can resume.

CASE STUDY: PHILIPPINES (MORO GULF), 1976	A tsunami and earthquake in the Cotabato Trench in the Celebes Sea killed more than 8,000 people in the Philippines in August 1976. Around 90% of the deaths were caused by the tsunami, which swept away the whole of Pagadian City while the population slept. Pagadian has been rebuilt. Most of the houses along the coast in Pagadian are made of wood, often supported on stilts. They were quick to rebuild, but are vulnerable to further tsunamis.

DID YOU KNOW? In some places, the floodwaters of the Japanese tsunami of 2011 reached 10 km (6 mi) inland.

Tsunami detection buoys float in the ocean and detect underwater earthquakes.

Using the survey, Japan's government planned to make "tsunami-safe cities" to protect from future disasters.

People are warned using sirens and public address systems. Places vulnerable to tsunamis often have signs showing people where to go in an emergency.

Tsunami Warning

Local early warning systems detect signs of earthquakes and Earth's plates shifting to predict a possible tsunami. People are warned using sirens and public address systems. Remote warning systems use wave gauges and seafloor pressure gauges to spot a sudden rise in sea level or rise in pressure on the seabed. The data can then be used to create accurate predictions and warnings.

What Is a Hurricane?

A hurricane is a furious, spinning tropical storm system that can smash buildings apart and hurl trees, cars, and massive chunks of debris far into the air. Wind speeds in a hurricane can reach more than 250 kph (155 mph). The wind brings with it torrential rain, thunder, and lightning. A hurricane roars in from the ocean and lashes the coast for hours causing terrible damage, but it dies down quite quickly as it moves farther inland.

In December 2021, Typhoon Rai hit the Philippines, causing devastation.

Hurricanes in History

Hurricanes have always happened, but because many strike areas where people did not keep written records, we do not have detailed accounts of them going back very far in time. As soon as Europeans began to visit South and Central America, they encountered hurricanes. Christopher Columbus's ship sheltered from a hurricane in a bay in 1502, but 20 other ships were sunk by the storm on their way back to Spain.

CASE STUDY: THE GREAT HURRICANE, 1780

Three hurricanes struck the West Indies in 1780, the worst of which killed 22,000 people over eight days, making it the deadliest hurricane ever to strike the western hemisphere. It destroyed nearly every building in Barbados, flattened St. Lucia, demolished St. Pierre (the capital of Martinique), and on St. Vincent it created a storm surge 6 m (19 ft) high that washed villages out to sea. Most of the British fleet at St. Lucia was sunk, as well as 15 Dutch ships in Grenada. It would be 200 years before another hurricane would claim more than 10,000 lives in the Atlantic.

Weather satellites show us a hurricane between Florida, USA, and Cuba.

Hurricane, *typhoon*, and *cyclone* are different names for the same weather event know in scientific terms as a "tropical cyclone." These storms have different names, depending on where they happen.

DID YOU KNOW? A severe tropical storm can be officially classed as a hurricane, typhoon, or cyclone if it has winds that blow faster than 119 kph (74 mph).

Where Hurricanes Happen

Tropical storms occur in tropical regions of the Atlantic, Indian, and Pacific Oceans. The water temperature must be at least 26.5 °C (79.7 °F) for the storm to be able to gather enough strength to be classed as a hurricane. Most Atlantic hurricanes form off the west coast of Africa, then drift westward to reach land in Central America and the Caribbean.

Hurricanes can damage essential services such as power and communication lines.

Powerful Storms

When a tropical cyclone reaches land, it wreaks destruction along the coast and continues its path inland. After hitting land, the storm rapidly loses power because it is no longer heated from beneath by tropical seas. Within 12 hours, most of the force has been spent—though it can travel as far as 280 km (175 mi) inland before dying out.

The most destructive hurricanes strike the southeastern coast of the United States, Central America, and the Caribbean. Cyclones plague the coasts around the Indian Ocean, most often striking Indonesia, India, Sri Lanka, and Thailand, but they also hit Madagascar and east Africa. In the Pacific, typhoons form around Japan, eastern China, and the Philippines, but they can also strike the west coast of Australia and New Guinea. Their impact is greatest in areas where most people live.

DID YOU KNOW? The word *hurricane* probably comes from the Taino people of Central America, whose "god of the storm" was named hurakán.

When tropical storms reach the land, they can do huge damage to buildings.

Jupiter's red spot is a giant, long-lived storm system.

GREATEST STORM IN THE SOLAR SYSTEM

The planet Jupiter has a large spot that is actually a massive storm system. Like a hurricane, it consists of winds whirling in a circle at great speeds up to 650 kph (400 mph). Jupiter is a gas giant—a planet made entirely of gas—so the storm will never drift over land and die down. The storm has been raging for at least 150 years and possibly more than 350 years. The storm is 24,800 km (154,100 mi) across, covering about the same area as Earth's entire surface.

How Hurricanes Happen

A tropical storm builds up over the sea where equatorial winds from different directions meet. The warm air spirals upward, taking heat and moisture from the sea and growing increasingly strong.

Drawing Power from the Sea

An Atlantic hurricane begins as a thunderstorm off the west coast of Africa and then becomes a tropical depression. This is a system of swirling clouds and rain, with winds of less than 62 kph (38 mph). Warm air, carrying evaporated water, rises from the surface of the sea. The air cools as it rises, and the water (in its gas form) condenses to form rain clouds, which add to the growing storm. Heat escapes from the condensing water and warms the air higher up, which rises in turn, setting up a cycle of warm air being sucked up from the ocean, losing its water to storm clouds, and warming more air. The rising column pulls ever more warm air and water from the surface of the sea.

Hurricane from 119 kph (74 mph)

Dense cold air

Cloudless eye of the storm

Air pushed out and back in

Rising humid air

Rain

Water temperature 26°C (79°F)

Colliding Winds

Winds from different directions collide and circle around the column of rising air and moisture, setting up a circular wind pattern. Much higher up, a stronger wind blowing in a single direction carries the warm air away, which in turn pulls up yet more air. High air pressure above the storm helps to suck in more air at the bottom where the air pressure is low. The wind speed increases, first to tropical storm strength—63 kph (39 mph)—and finally to hurricane force—119 kph (74 mph) or above.

DID YOU KNOW? Some tropical cyclone clouds are so thick, they can cause near darkness on the Earth below.

In 2018, Hurricane Michael, began as a small tropical storm in the Caribbean. It moved into the Gulf of Mexico and grew to become a category 5 hurricane.

The storm surge caused huge damage along the US coast.

A tornado swirls across Nebraska, USA. Most tornadoes form over the Great Plains of the USA.

TORNADOES

Tornadoes are small, rapidly circling whirlwinds. They may travel ahead of hurricanes, or in their wake (behind them), but they can also occur on their own, inland. A tornado forms beneath a storm cloud when air is sucked up into the storm cloud from the ground. Sometimes up to 3 km (2 mi) wide, a tornado can travel at 80 kph (50 mph) and have winds of up to 480 kph (300 mph). Rising warm air sucks in more air from beneath the tornado in the same way that happens in a hurricane.

Anatomy of a Hurricane

Hurricanes have a clear structure, and all hurricanes share the same characteristics.

Parts of a Hurricane

The destructive part of a hurricane is the whirling band of wind and rainstorms. In the middle of the storm is a still area with very low air pressure called the eye. A thick bank of cloud and rain just around the eye is called the eye wall. Outside the eye wall, there may be a moat—an area of reduced rain. A thin veil of very high cloud over the top of the hurricane system—made of tiny ice crystals—is called the veil of cirrus. The hurricane can extend 18 km (11 mi) upward. Widths vary, but a large hurricane is typically around 480 km (298 mi) wide—but can be larger.

Under Pressure

A hurricane is a low pressure system. The air in the middle of the storm is at very low pressure—indeed, the lowest air pressures recorded on Earth have been at the eye of a hurricane. Because the air pressure is so low, warm air and water are drawn up into the hurricane, continually feeding it.

A NASA computer model shows the astonishing track and forceful winds of Hurricane Sandy. A day before it hit the USA in 2012, Hurricane Sandy was nearly 1,850 km (1,150 mi) wide.

HURRICANE WINDS

Winds whip around in a hurricane at speeds of 160 to 250 kph (99 to 155 mph), or even over 320 kph (198 mph) in a very severe Pacific typhoon. Hurricane Wilma (2005) had the fastest winds recorded in an Atlantic hurricane at 295 kph (185 mph). The winds in a hurricane circle counterclockwise in the northern hemisphere and clockwise in the southern hemisphere. This is because of the effect of the spinning of the Earth on the movement of the wind and cloud.

DID YOU KNOW? In a category 5 hurricane, nearly all trees are likely to be uprooted or snapped, and almost all buildings blown down.

A thick bank of cloud and rain just around the eye is called the eye wall.

This image of Hurricane Florence was taken from the International Space Station. Florence hit in 2018. Over two days, it brought enormous rainfall to North and South Carolina, USA.

1 Minimal Damage	2 Moderate Damage	3 Extensive Damage	4 Extreme Damage	5 Catastrophic Damage
119–153 kph (74–95 mph)	154–177 kph (96–110 mph)	178–208 kph (111–129 mph)	209–251 kph (130–156 mph)	>252 kph (>157 mph)

Saffir-Simpson hurricane scale

The scale used for reporting the size of hurricanes is based on wind speed and the damage caused. The scale looks only at wind speed and does not take into account other dangers caused by hurricanes, such as storm surges, floods, and tornadoes.

The Saffir–Simpson hurricane scale shows wind speeds and damage.

Predictable Buildup

Hurricanes are part of the normal weather patterns that happen around the world each year. In the Atlantic, the hurricane season lasts from June to November.

Wind and Water

Every year, hot and cold winds blow at certain times and in certain places as part of the global weather pattern. There are also regular patterns to the temperatures of the sea in different areas. Hurricanes happen when certain patterns of wind and sea temperature occur at the same time. Meteorologists (people who study the weather) track wind speeds and study satellite photographs of weather systems to help them spot when a hurricane is brewing. They use computer techniques to predict the likely path of a growing hurricane.

This forecast shows where the hurricane is expected to travel.

Helping People to Safety

When a hurricane is expected, governments can warn people to take shelter or move to a safe area. Since weather systems are immensely complex and can change quickly, predictions are not always accurate. Scientists can only predict the wind speeds that will occur on land just before the hurricane hits the coast.

Sometimes, it is difficult for governments to decide whether to risk evacuating people needlessly or to leave them where they may be in danger. Evacuation can lead to road traffic accidents, and unnecessary evacuations can make people less likely to take notice of similar warnings in future.

DID YOU KNOW? If a hurricane is particularly bad or causes many deaths, its name is retired and replaced by a new name.

A satellite above Earth takes images and measurements of weather patterns.

Over the course of five days, Hurricane Irma grew to a category 5 hurricane, with winds as strong as 295 kph (185 mph).

HURRICANE NAMES

SInce 1953, hurricanes have been given human names. There are different sets of names in use around the world. For Atlantic hurricanes, a set of 21 names, each starting with a different letter of the alphabet, is available for use each year. As a hurricane is announced, it is given the next free name. If all the names are used up—if there are more than 21 hurricanes in a year—there is a list of extra names that can be used. Six lists of names are used in rotation.

Wild Winds and Water

Although a hurricane causes most damage to people once it hits land, its effects out at sea can be devastating to shipping. When it strikes the coast, the accompanying rain, flooding, and raging tides can sometimes cause more damage than the winds themselves.

As a hurricane approaches land, it brings wind, rain, and a storm surge that can flood waterfronts and beaches, and smash through storm barriers.

Out at Sea

All hurricanes start out at sea, and some travel great distances before reaching land. They can sink large and small boats, and it is difficult to use either rescue boats or helicopters to help shipwrecked sailors during a hurricane.

In the Air

Hurricanes would be very dangerous to aircraft, but there is usually enough warning for pilots to keep well away from them. Even so, strong winds far away from the hurricane itself can cause rough conditions. High winds can hamper emergency work, because rescue helicopters and planes carrying relief supplies cannot approach the disaster zone until the winds drop.

Tropical cyclone Winston hit the islands of Fiji in February 2016 causing catastrophe. It was one of the strongest storms recorded in the southern hemisphere.

Super Typhoons

Extra-strong typhoons, more powerful than any Atlantic hurricanes, are called super typhoons. With winds well over 240 kph (149 mph) and even as much as 320 kph (198 mph), the largest ever recorded was Super Typhoon Tip, which formed in the northwest Pacific in 1979. It was 2,220 km (1,380 mi) at its largest and had wind speeds of up to 305 kph (190 mph). Increasingly large and powerful hurricanes, called hypercanes by scientists, are expected in the Atlantic, too, as global weather conditions change.

Mexico Beach in Florida, USA, was severely damaged by the storm surge caused by Hurricane Michael in 2018.

CASE STUDY: HAKATA BAY, 1281

In 1281, a great typhoon destroyed the invasion fleet that the Mongol leader Kublai Kahn had assembled to attack Japan. It ripped through Hakata Bay in southwest Japan, sinking nearly 2,000 of the fleet of 2,200, and drowning between 45,000 and 65,000 troops. An earlier invasion fleet had met the same fate in 1274, with the loss of 13,000 men. The Japanese gave the Hakata Bay typhoon the name *Kamikaze*, meaning "divine wind," because it seemed as though the gods had sent it to save them.

Riding the Storm

The approach of a hurricane is terrifying for people who live near the coast. Even though hurricanes happen every year, each one usually hits a fairly small strip of coast, so most people do not see many large hurricanes.

On the Beach

The storm surge is the first part of a hurricane to strike land. Waves can be up to 13 m (42 ft) high, washing over quays and beachfronts and battering through storm barriers and sea walls. The waves tear boats from their moorings and smash them against walls, or even carry them far inland.

As the wind makes its way over the beach, it whips up the sand into a cloud. Sometimes, the sand can become electrically charged in the storm clouds and glow with static electricity.

Violent Winds

The winds grow in strength, often bringing torrential rain at the same time. Houses sometimes explode, because the pressure inside them is much higher than the pressure outside. People may be blown over, smashed into objects, or picked up by the wind and carried some distance before they are dropped.

After time, the wind calms and many people think the danger is over. But this is the eye of the hurricane passing, and the storm soon restarts as violently as before. People who come out from shelter when the eye passes over them are often caught unawares by the second wind.

Hurricane Irma affected the US states of Florida, Georgia, and Alabama, bringing down trees and power lines, that blocked roads and caused loss of power.

If people know that a hurricane is coming, they can take precautions such as boarding up windows.

Even when Hurricane Irma began to weaken, the tropical storm winds still stretched 684 km (425 mi) across.

CASE STUDY: HURRICANE MITCH, 1998

Hurricane Mitch ripped through Honduras and Nicaragua in 1998. It first hit land as a tropical storm in Florida but gathered strength as it passed over the sea again. Torrential rains caused flooding and mudslides, killing 11,000 people and making it the most deadly hurricane since the Great Hurricane of 1780. The flooding was made worse by the slow movement of the hurricane over land, which gave plenty of time for rain to fall.

DID YOU KNOW? Following the terrible aftermath of Hurricane Mitch, the name was retired and will not be used again.

People in Danger

Many people fear the winds of a hurricane, but most deaths are caused by flooding and the aftermath of the storm.

Mozambique experienced two cyclones just five weeks apart in 2019. Heavy rains brought floods, landslides, and power failure.

Immediate Dangers

People caught in a hurricane are in danger from the high winds that can carry objects through the air, damage buildings, or even pull people up into the air. Hurricanes are often accompanied by floods from the sea, from rivers bursting their banks, and from torrential rain.

After the Storm

Even when the winds die down, the danger is not over. The land may stay flooded for weeks. People may have nowhere to shelter from continuing bad weather and no food or clean water. Injured and sick people are often cut off from medical help. Survivors may begin to suffer from exposure if the weather is cold; or they may suffer dehydration, sunstroke, or heat exhaustion if it is hot. In some areas, they may be prey to poisonous snakes, dangerous animals, and disease-carrying insects.

In refugee camps and emergency accommodation, people are often crowded together in conditions without adequate food, water, or medical attention.

CASE STUDY: GALVESTON, 1900

The hurricane that hit the island of Galveston, Texas, USA, in September 1900, caused the worst natural disaster in US history. With winds of up to 235 kph (145 mph) and a storm surge of 3.7 m (12 ft), it killed more than 6,000 people and destroyed 3,600 homes. With no early warning systems or tracking technology, the people of Galveston did not know that the hurricane was coming and were not evacuated.

In 2013, Super Typhoon Haiyan (also Yolanda) hit the islands of the Philippines. Communities were destroyed, and emergency aid was needed.

Hurricane Harvey brought flooding to Texas, USA, in 2017.

Around 4 million people were displaced by Typhoon Haiyan. Once rescue efforts have been made, cleaning up the waste and debris begins.

DID YOU KNOW? Often, more people drown in floods than are killed by the winds. In some areas, floods can lead to deadly mudslides and landslides.

Helping Out

When a hurricane strikes an inhabited area, help of many kinds is needed immediately. Often, local emergency services cannot cope with the demand, and national, and sometimes international, aid from governments and charities is needed.

Immediate Tasks

The most urgent work for rescue groups and emergency services is to free people who are trapped or who are cut off by floodwaters, and to move injured people to safety. Whether they are injured or not, survivors need emergency housing, medical supplies, food, and water.

It is important to remove dead bodies from the disaster zone, too, as their presence is not only upsetting for survivors but soon leads to disease. Bodies decaying in water that provides drinking supplies can cause outbreaks of gastroenteritis, which may be deadly when treatment and clean water are not available.

Cut Off

It can be very difficult for help to reach the disaster area. Even without flooding, debris can block or destroy roads, train lines, and ports, making it impossible for people to move out of the area or for help to reach them. Landslides or mudslides may destroy key bridges and roads. If strong winds and rain continue after the hurricane, planes and helicopters may not be usable.

It is important for basic food supplies to reach people who are stranded after natural disasters.

CASE STUDY: HURRICANE KATRINA, 2005

Hurricane Katrina struck New Orleans on the Gulf Coast of the United States in August 2005. It broke the levees (walls that hold back the lake and river behind the city), and around 80% of the city was flooded. Thousands of people were encouraged to make their way to sports stadiums and conference venues for temporary shelter. But these venues lacked electricity, sanitation, air conditioning, and sufficient food and water. Local and federal government were heavily criticized for their handling of the disaster.

More than a million people were evacuated to safer areas before Cyclone Phailin struck the Indian coast.

DID YOU KNOW? Even minor injuries can be fatal because wading through sewage and mud can cause wounds to become infected.

After the Storm

In the days and weeks following a hurricane, the extent of the damage to people's lives as well as to property slowly emerges. Whole families may have been killed, communities destroyed, and people's lives changed for ever.

Cleaning Up

As soon as a hurricane is over, local, national, and international teams start rebuilding road and train links, so that emergency workers can reach people who are trapped or stranded. They may need to clear debris, drain or pump out floodwater and rebuild sea walls or levees to protect the area from further damage by other hurricanes and winds. They also need to demolish unsafe buildings and clear the land.

Devastated Communities

Many people lose not only their homes but family members and friends when a catastrophic hurricane strikes. For them, life will never be the same again. When many people have suffered the same fate, it may seem as though the community itself can never be rebuilt. In addition, the area may be left without essential amenities such as water, electricity, schools, hospitals, shops, and transportation systems. These can take years to rebuild.

Rebuilding homes

DID YOU KNOW? Planners and engineers can design buildings that will be safer, but making stormproof buildings can be very expensive.

Damage following Hurricane Michael was estimated at $25 billion. It will take years to rebuild.

CORAL REEFS IN DANGER

In Samoa and other Pacific islands, coral reefs are often damaged by typhoons. The large waves whipped up by a typhoon batter the reef, breaking off chunks that may have taken centuries to grow. The sea carries broken lumps of coral into island lagoons where they crash into inland reefs. Topsoil washed from islands into the sea cuts off sunlight to the reef, preventing plant growth. The nutrients in the soil encourage algae to grow in the sea, further disturbing the fragile balance of the reef.

Glossary

AFTERSHOCK The shaking of the ground as it settles down after an earthquake.

ASH CLOUD A large cloud of ash blown into the air by a volcano.

BOUNDARY Where the edges of two tectonic plates meet, also called a fault.

CALDERA A giant dip in the ground or on the seabed, formed when the ground collapses into the empty magma chamber of a volcano.

CONDENSE Make droplets of liquid from a gas by cooling.

CONVECTION A movement of heat by air or water currents.

CRATER A bowl-shaped dip in the top of a volcano.

DEBRIS Trash and broken items.

DELTA A fan-shaped area of land formed by sediment where a river meets the sea.

DORMANT Inactive but not dead.

DROUGHT A period of time when there is little or no rainfall.

EROSION The wearing away of rock and soil by natural forces, such as running water.

ERUPTION The ejection of hot, semiliquid rock, gas, and/or ash by a volcano.

EVACUATE Leave an area because of danger.

EVAPORATE Change from a liquid to a gas.

FAULT / FAULTLINE A boundary between two or more tectonic plates.

FOCUS The point underground where an earthquake originates.

FORESHOCK The shaking of the ground that comes before the main movement of an earthquake.

GLACIER A slow-moving river of ice that flows down a valley.

HYDROELECTRICITY Electricity generated by turbines that are powered by flowing water.

INFRASTRUCTURE Roads, bridges, train lines, sewage systems, and other large public structures.

IRRIGATION The supply of water to farmland for watering crops.

LANDSLIDE A slippage of a large mass of rock or earth.

LEVEE An embankment alongside a river or the coast, built to prevent flooding of the surrounding land.

MAGMA Molten rock inside Earth's crust.

MANTLE A layer of Earth formed of semiliquid, moving, molten rock (magma).

MEANDER A long, looping bend of a river across its floodplain.

MONSOON A seasonal period of heavy rain common in some tropical areas with a particular weather pattern.

MUD FLOW A fast-moving mixture of ash and water.

PRECIPITATION Rain, sleet, snow, or hail.

PYROCLASTIC FLOW A thick cloud of red-hot ash and rock that pours rapidly down the side of a volcano.

RESERVOIR A large area of water collected as a water supply for people.

SATURATED Containing so much water that no more can be soaked up.

SEISMIC WAVE A wave of energy released by earthquake activity.

SILT Sediment made up of very tiny pieces of rock.

TECTONIC PLATE One of the giant pieces that make up Earth's crust.

TOPSOIL The nutrient-rich layer of soil in which plants grow.

TROPICAL Relating to the tropics, the areas just above and below the equator.

TROPICAL CYCLONE An intense storm system that develops over the ocean.

Index

acid rain 81
Africa 88, 108
aftershocks 14, 21–3
agriculture 42–3, 52, 60, 77, 81, 85
aid 100–1, 122–3
air pressure 34, 112
Amazon rain forest 52, 60
Anak Krakatau 67, 92–3
animals 19, 57–8
Antioch, Syria 15
Armenia 25, 57
ash 58, 65–6, 70, 72, 74–82, 84
Atacama Trench 9
Atlantic Ocean 69, 108, 110, 112, 114–15, 117
Australia 50, 52, 57, 86, 108

Bangladesh 31, 43
Biblical flood 27
Boscastle, UK 33
Brazil 40, 70–1

calderas 70, 78
Camp Fire, California 55
Caribbean 106, 108, 111
Central America 12, 84, 106, 108
Chile 7, 80
China 12, 19, 21, 31, 108
cities 6–7, 12–13, 15, 17, 19, 21–3, 25, 32, 34–5, 44, 94, 96–7, 103–5
cloudburst 32
Colorado, USA 62–3
combustion 49, 50
continental drift 10
coral reefs 125
Crater Lake, Oregon 78
crops 42–3, 60, 81
crust 6, 8–9, 11, 14, 68, 90, 92
Cyclone Phailin 122–3

dams 38–9, 44–5
deposition 40
disease 36, 37, 99, 122
drought 50, 57, 60

earthquakes 4, 6–25, 77, 79
    epicenter 14, 16, 18, 21
Ecuador 15
eruption columns 74–5
Etna, Mount 81
Eurasian Plate 12, 68
Europe 10, 16, 29, 88
Everest, Mount 11
Everglades National Park 51

Fagradalsfjall volcano 69
Fairweather Fault system 89
fire 15, 22, 23, 46–65
firefighters 47–9, 53, 55–6, 64–5
flood barriers 44–5
floodplains 26–7, 29, 42–5
floods 4, 26–45, 82–3, 120–2
    coastal 26, 34–5, 44, 86–7, 96, 116, 119–20
    flash 26, 29, 32–3, 36, 40–1
    river 26, 28–32, 36–7, 40, 42–5, 120
foreshocks 14, 18, 20
forest fires (wildfires) 5, 46–65
France 51
Fuji, Mount 70, 77

Galveston 120
Great East Japan earthquake 86, 89, 96–7, 101
Great Hurricane 1780 106, 119
Greece 56–7, 63–5, 83, 86, 88
Guwahati, India 31

Hakata Bay typhoon 117
Hawaii 69, 73, 76, 80, 88
Himalayas 10–11
Hurricane Florence 113
Hurricane Irma 114–15, 118–19
Hurricane Katrina 34, 123
Hurricane Michael 111, 117, 125
Hurricane Mitch 119
hurricanes 4, 34, 106–25
hydropower 38–9

ice caps 82
Iceland 9, 68–9, 72, 82
India 22, 31, 99, 108
Indian Ocean 16–17, 108
Indian Ocean tsunami 90–1, 99–103
Indonesia 17, 52, 66, 74, 81, 90, 94–5, 98, 108
island arcs 76
islands, volcanic 76
Italy 16, 57, 66, 70, 81, 84, 88

Japan 7, 12–13, 19, 39, 70, 77, 86, 89, 104, 108, 117
Jupiter 109

Kea, Mount 76
Kilauea 73
Kobe 13
Krakatau 66–7, 92
Kurobe Dam, Japan 39

lahars 79, 82–3
land clearance 52
landslides 40–1, 87, 89–90, 121–2
lava 66, 70, 72–3, 76–7, 80, 82, 84
lightning 46–7, 50–1, 59
Lisbon, Portugal 91
Lituya Bay 89

magma 66, 68–74, 78–9, 82, 92
mantle 8, 9, 68
Mayon volcano 85
Mazama, Mount 78
Mediterranean Sea 16, 88
meteorites 86–7
Mid-Atlantic Ridge 68–9
Modified Mercalli Intensity Scale 20–1
Monserrat 82–3
monsoons 30–1, 42
mountains 69, 76–7
Mozambique 37, 120
mudflows 79, 82–3
mudslides 119, 121–2

Nazca plate 9, 15
Nepal 7, 31
Netherlands 29, 35, 44
New Orleans 34, 123
North America 10, 50, 78
North Sea 44

Oosterscheldekering 44–5

Pacific Ocean 9, 12, 69, 73, 88, 90, 98, 108, 112, 117, 125
Pacific Plate 12
paddies 42
Pagadian City 104
Palu, Indonesia 17, 94–5, 98
Pangaea 10–11
Papua New Guinea 103
Paricutín, Mexico 77
Philippines 75, 85, 104, 106, 108, 121
Pinatubo, Mount 75
Piva National Park 54
Port-au-Prince, Haiti 24–5
Portugal 63, 91
pyroclastic flows 74, 76, 80, 82, 84

rainfall 29–32, 37, 50, 81, 81–2, 110, 112–13, 116, 119, 122
rescue workers 22–3, 25, 100–1, 122–3
reservoirs 38, 44
Richter scale 20–1
Ring of Fire 12, 94
rock, igneous 76
runoff 28, 41

Saffir-Simpson hurricane scale 113
St. Francis Dam failure 39

St. Helens, Mount 78–9, 81
San Andreas Fault 14, 23
San Francisco 6, 23
seamounts 69, 76
sediment 40
seismic waves 14, 16
seismographs 18
slash-and-burn 52, 60
smoke jumpers 64
snow melt 30, 82
soil 27, 84
    erosion 26, 40–1, 58
South America 12, 22, 77, 106
Spain 45, 106
Spitak, Armenia 25
spontaneous combustion 50
storm surges 34, 36, 43–4, 111, 116–18, 120
storms 4, 30, 32–5, 37, 43, 82, 106–25
Sugarloaf Mountain 70–1
Sumbawa 81

Tambora 81
Tangshan, China 21
tectonic plate boundaries/faults 8–12, 14–16, 23, 68–9, 88–90
Thames Flood Barrier 44–5
thunderstorms 33, 82
tornadoes 111
tropical cyclones 30, 34, 37, 43, 107, 110, 120
tsunami 4–5, 7, 16–17, 19, 26, 34, 36, 83, 86–105
tuff 76, 84
Turkey 23, 57
Typhoon Haiyan 121
typhoons 106–7, 125
    super 117, 121

United States 6, 12, 14, 23, 31, 33–4, 49, 51, 53, 55, 59, 62–3, 78–9, 88, 108, 111, 113, 117–21, 123

Venice 35
Vesuvius, Mount 70, 84–5
Volcano Fuego, Guatemala 66–7
volcanoes 5, 9, 12, 50, 66–85
    cinder cones 72–3
    composite cone (stratovolcanoes) 70–1, 82
    explosive 74–5, 78–9, 92
    hotspot 69, 72
    Plinian eruptions 74
    shield 72–3
    status 70

water cycle 28
wave trains 97
wildfires 46–65
wind 54–5, 57, 63, 106–7, 110, 112, 114–16, 118–20, 122

Yellowstone National Park 59, 78